THE MYTHMAKERS

OHIO UNIVERSITY PRESS · ATHENS, OHIO

THE MYTHMAKERS

MARY BARNARD

Acknowledgments

I am especially indebted to Mr. R. Gordon Wasson, Mrs. Maud Worcester Makemson, and Mr. R. F. Arragon, who have read portions of the manuscript, offered encouragement, and preserved me from certain errors.

Two chapters, "A Dragon Hunt" and "The God in the Flowerpot," were first published in *The American Scholar*.

M. B.

TO MY PARENTS, WITH LOVE AND GRATITUDE

Contents

PART I

1)   How to make a mythomorph

I have been reading a great deal recently about the
origins of myth *—origins in ritual, in folktale, in history,
in metaphor, in the unconscious or preconscious psyche,
and so on. I have read about mythopoeic periods, the
mythopoeic mentality, and the function of myth in the
social structure. The scope of the discussion is so wide,
and the material is so intangible that a mind like mine
loses its way in a wilderness of generalities. Perhaps
there are others who are as confused as I am; for their
benefit and my own I have attempted to isolate just
one aspect of one problem bearing on the nature and

* Sources of comments on terms and personages under discussion are
gathered, with suggestions for further reading, by chapter and by
page, after page 184. The terms discussed are not marked in the text.

origin of myths: that is, the origin of a few mythical personae—deities or others—related to a single familiar theme: intoxication. These inventions, or mythomorphs, are especially apt to my purpose because speculation is cut to a minimum; we know what the myth "means," and we have a clue to its origins. For the moment, let us ignore the theories and proceed with the myths.

My first example is the Aztec goddess Mayauel, who is identified with the maguey plant. Before we can talk intelligently about Mayauel we need to know a few facts about her vegetable incarnation. For instance, the maguey (*Agave Americana*) is especially valued for its sap, from which the Indians make a mildly intoxicating beverage called pulque. These Indians live in arid country where any potable liquid has its uses; however, pulque is also a source of vitamins generally lacking in the diet of the pulque drinkers. The maguey cannot be tapped every year like a sugar maple, but only at one stage of its growth, when it is eight to ten or twelve years old. Later the central stalk sends up a shoot and the plant is of no further use to the pulquemakers. When the maguey is ripe for tapping, the heart is cut out of the plant with a special knife, the operation being referred to as "castration." For six months thereafter the sap is collected twice a day. Some of the sap is fermented to the point of putrefaction. This is the "pulque seed." Various roots are added either to the liquor itself or to the seed to increase its power of intoxication. The resulting beverage is white, thick, sweet, nourishing, and about as intoxicating as beer.

Mayauel, the deified maguey, is frequently pictured in the Aztec codices. For instance, in the *Codex Laud* she is seated on a snake and tortoise throne in the midst of a maguey that is ripe for tapping. She is naked and brandishes a knife of the sort used for piercing the plant;

again she is a naked woman seated in the plant and suckling a child. Her husband was Patecatl, called "He from the Land of Medicines." He is a god of medicine; also he is identified with a plant used in making pulque, and he rules the Grass day-names in the Aztec calendar. The texts say that Mayauel's sons are the 400 Rabbits, all of whom are pulque gods, and that she nurses them at her four hundred breasts. Drunkenness is measured in Middle America even today by numbers of rabbits, 400 Rabbits being considered the last, highest or lowest, degree of drunkenness.

Bearing Mayauel in mind, let us look at a definition of mythology according to Jungian theory: "Myths are original revelations of the pre-conscious psyche, involuntary statements about unconscious happenings, and anything but allegories of physical processes."

There is no hint anywhere that Mayauel was invented before pulque was invented, and the process of pulque-making could hardly have been discovered by a pre-conscious psyche. The Jungian answer to that observation would surely be that Mayauel as a Great Mother archetype was already floating in the collective unconscious, waiting to be fitted to the maguey when pulque was invented. I confess I do not know anything about the unconscious minds of the Aztec mythmakers, but I have two pertinent questions.

The first question is, what other personification would be appropriate? The mythmaker had a choice between human and animal (including birds, reptiles and fishes). If he chose the human, he had a choice between male and female, and a choice of ages. The maguey might have been personified as a child, or a young man, or an old man or woman. The important fact here is that the maguey was prized for its white, milky sap (like that of rubber trees, which are also "milked"). If the Aztecs had

had milch cows they might have personified the maguey as a cow; however, in their society only children drank milk, and the only milk they drank was mother's milk. Mayauel is therefore a nursing mother, or wetnurse; she is not inevitably a human female of childbearing age, but the odds were in favor of precisely that personification. Palm trees tapped by people who use their sap for palm wine have also been personified, if not deified, as women who give a precious milk.

My second question is, if all the representations of Mayauel had been stamped in clay and buried in desert sand for three thousand years, and then excavated, what label would she bear? For the last fifty years and more, any female deity definitely associated with a plant, no matter what plant, would have been described as a vegetation goddess; and if the same goddess were sometimes shown nursing a child, she would have fallen into the category of fertility goddess and Great Mother as well. The merest suggestion of a rabbit, let alone four hundred of them, would have clinched the matter for the fertility ritualists, while the numerous breasts would have identified her as a Great Mother. But in the case of Mayauel and the maguey, we know the plant, we know what drink was made from it, and how it was (and is) made. We know Mayauel's connection with the pulque gods and the calendar. She is nowhere identified with vegetation in general, nor with fertility in general, but only with the maguey. In the case of the older plant goddesses, where we often do not know the associations, each mythologist is free to see in them (as the mental patient sees in the Rorschach ink–blot) any significance he likes to find there. The identification he makes will tell us something about the mythologist, and next to nothing about the mythmaker or the origin of the myth.

Mayauel has a male counterpart in the god Soma of the Hindus. Although he is very old indeed—one of the oldest deities in the Hindu pantheon—his incarnation in a plant is as specific as Mayauel's. The Hindus used their soma drink, as the Aztecs used their pulque, on ceremonial occasions. The plant called soma in their literature has not been identified and may even be extinct, but no one has ever suggested that it was imaginary. Although the drink made from the plant was an intoxicant, it seems not to have been fermented. This places it in the same category (roughly) with the ceremonial kava drink of the South Seas and the jimsonweed drink (toloache) of our California Indians. The stalks or roots were pounded in mortars and mixed with water, then wrung or strained out of the liquid which was drunk as a ceremonial beverage. The Hindus mixed soma juice with milk.

One hundred fourteen hymns making up the whole of the ninth book of the *Rig Veda* are dedicated to Soma, who is both plant and drink personified. They are mainly "incantations sung over the tangible soma while it is pressed by the stones, flows through the woolen strainer into the wooden vats, in which it is finally offered on a litter of grass to the gods as a beverage, sometimes in fire, or drunk by the priests." The preparation of the nectar was as much a rite as its consumption, and equally celebrated by the poets. From the hymns we learn that the plant grew on the mountains; the shoots or stalks were steeped in water before they were crushed and wrung out in the woolen strainer. The juice extracted was then mixed with milk, sour milk and barley. In the poet's metaphor, the milk and barley became the "god's garments"; the ten fingers that squeeze the strainer are ten maidens, and the stalks are udders giving milk. In the early period the stalks were laid on a hide and macerated with stones. Later they were crushed with the ceremonial mortar and pestle. The god, that is, was crushed, and the god was drunk in liquid form. He is credited with giving strength to the arm of the warrior; he is charioteer to the war god; he inspires poets and seers. He is a personified power, his functions being those of the intoxicating drink called by the same name. He *is* the drink.

While we know a good deal about Mayauel and Soma, we have no account of the actual shaping of a drink-plant mythomorph. If we want to answer the question that comes to mind immediately—*Why* a deity?—Why should an intoxicant be raised to godhood?—we shall do well to turn again not to modern theory, whether philosophical, psychological or theological, but to the origins and cult uses of intoxicating drinks so far as these are known.

No man who was totally unacquainted with fermented beverages ever said to himself, "Now I shall make some beer. We need it for our next religious festival." The discovery of fermentation must have been accidental. To account for the origin of their algarroba (carob) beer, the Toba Indians of Brazil tell a little story plausible enough to be history although it introduces their cycle of myths. They say that there was once a stubborn man who refused to eat his algarroba mush. His equally stubborn wife refused to cook more for him until he had eaten what she gave him. Meanwhile the rejected mush stood in its dish before the door of their hut. After some days the wife's father tasted the mush to find out whether, as the husband said, it was unfit to eat. He found it delicious. He called another man, who also approved. More water was added, and more friends were called to taste the mush. Soon they all became quite drunk, laughing and shouting. "They said, 'Tomorrow we shall go get more algarroba husks and we shall make more beer.' They pounded the husks, put them in big calabashes with water. By midnight the beverage was fermenting. At dawn it was sour (that is to say, fermented). Then they drank. The women drank too."

The Tobas do not tell us what happened the next day, and the next. Did they go on getting drunk as often as possible and staying drunk until the beer was gone? Did they fall to fighting among themselves? Did their enemies surprise them as they lay in a drunken stupor? Whatever may have happened to bring the impromptu first orgy to a halt, the investigator will find that most savages use their intoxicants ceremonially and only on stated occasions. People who have no vessels in which to seal their beer cannot store it in their cellars for private drinking when they feel in the mood for it. They brew their fermented drinks in old canoes, hides, or hollow logs, and they drink until the improvised cauldron is empty. The neighbors are not only invited, they help with collecting the honey or carob pods and brewing the drink. They sing, dance, jingle deer hooves or beat drums "to hasten fermentation" or at least to allay their impatience and help to pass the time until the brew is ready. They drink for births and marriages and deaths. They drink to start a war or end one. They drink to install a chief, to celebrate the New Year, to honor the gods, to consult the oracles, to make rain, to make the corn grow, and so on. It might be possible to fill a book with examples of ceremonies in which intoxicants are used for one magical reason or another. Yet, as I have pointed out, they must have been discovered accidentally. Brewing methods were surely perfected be-

cause intoxication was pleasant, in fact so pleasant that
the use and brewing of beer or mead had to be limited
to ceremonial drinkfests. In societies where religion and
social organization are inseparable, and every authorized
carousal is by association religious, the drinkfest was
almost certain to become a religious ceremony. Suppose that only churches were licensed to brew and dispense beer, and even the church was allowed to dispense
it only on Sundays, and, further, that the beer had to be
consumed on the premises: this is more or less the situation that prevailed among the Polynesians and South
Americans until the European appeared with his bottled
liquor. The Abipones of the Gran Chaco restricted themselves to ceremonial drinking, but they were so much
given to drunkenness that they managed to circumvent
their own restrictions by having a drinkfest for every
name-giving, and changing their names "as Europeans
do their clothes."

The ceremonial use of intoxicants is one factor in the
deification of the drink plant or drug plant, but the
power of the intoxicant is of course another. Whether it
induces a state of euphoria or incites to acts of violence,
the drinker is "possessed." There is still a third: even at
its lowest level the drinkfest is likely to be a songfest as
well. Francis Huxley has described the drinkfest of another Brazilian tribe, the Urubus, who drink cauín (from
kau, drunk, crazy, and *i,* water). "They start drinking,"
he says, "as the sun sets, and go on all through the night,
singing as they do in praise of the cauín: singing about
manioc tubers pounded in the trough, manioc mash put
through the sieve, manioc made into pancakes and
baked in the oven, manioc pancakes fermenting in pots
into cauín." After drinking all night they were "puri-
fied" and ready to begin their ceremonies. Huxley says

nothing of personification or deification of the cauín, although he does say that the Urubus conceive of alcohol as a "spirit" which possesses them when they are drunk. If, in their songs, they had addressed themselves directly to this spirit, their manioc beer would have been on its way to deification. "To address, one must personify," says Elizabeth Bowen of the poets who have addressed Rome; drinkers and brewers of drink who address their tipple directly in song must also personify; if the tipple is used in religious ceremonies, its sacred character is already established, and godhood is only one step away.

Some people are more given to personification than others; some are more given to metaphor. The Hindus over a long period of time created an elaborate mythomorph and an elaborate ritual whereas the Urubus were content to sing about their cauín simply as a beverage without turning it into a god. The body of a Tahitian chief, drunk on kava, was said to be possessed by a god, yet the Polynesians seem never to have personified their ceremonial drink. Kava, however, like soma, was the drink of the gods, and pulque, like soma, was the drink of the ancestors. All were poured in libations, drunk by priests when they communed with the gods, and used regularly in important ceremonies. All, for one reason or another, were hedged round with restrictions on their preparation and use.

Soma and Mayauel have been identified for us by the mythmakers themselves; the only problem they present to the mythologist, besides the one I have just discussed, is the question of fitting them into his system. Do they agree with his definition of myth and his theory of myth origins? And if they do not, are they therefore to be ruled out of the discussion? If we rule out Soma and

Mayauel, what shall we do about Bacchus? If we rule out the known, what do we do about the unknown? When is a myth not a myth?

As a final example, take the story of Kvasir as related by Snorri in the *Prose Edda*. In this Icelandic tale (presumably traditional), it is said that Kvasir was created at peacemaking ceremonies when the gods gathered together and spit into a vessel. Kvasir was born of the spittle. The gods gave him all wisdom, so that no matter what question was asked of him, Kvasir had a ready answer. Eventually, two dwarfs overcame him by trickery. They killed him and drained his blood into two vats and a tub, mixed it with honey, and from this concoction brewed the Mead of the Poets, called Odrörir.

The spittle from which Kvasir was born is the key to this story. Primitive brewers all over the world have known how to use the enzymes in saliva to encourage fermentation. For this reason the Indians of Brazil chewed the grain used in making maize beer, and spit it into a container of water where it was left to ferment. Neighboring Indians chewed honeycomb for their honey drink, and algarroba pods for algarroba beer. When the festival beer is made by this process, the chewing and spitting become part of the ceremony, the chewers and spitters being a select group of old women, high-born virgins or young boys. Knowing that the ceremonial use of beer in peacemaking is widespread, and, further, that spitting into a vessel can be an important preliminary to the brewing process, I asked myself when I read this story whether the Norse mythmakers were familiar with the use of spittle in brewing. I soon found the answer in another story of a beer-brewing contest between two women, one of whom asked Odin for help. The god gave her some of his spittle to use instead of yeast "and so she made the best beer in the world."

When I investigated still further, I found that Jacob Grimm and Andrew Lang were before me; Grimm, in fact, relates the name Kvasir to the drink called kvass. Lang compares the Norse hero to John Barleycorn. It would seem, then, that the riddle of Kvasir would have been no mystery at all to the original audiences, but it would have tickled them; riddles were a favorite form of Icelandic poetry. The tale is surely not a description of a cannibalistic blood-drinking rite. It is a metaphor. Yet some mythologists deny that myths are ever metaphors, and in that case the story of Kvasir is not a myth at all. Very likely it is not. But, if we grant that Soma is a myth, although Kvasir is only a metaphor, we surely must agree that some myths and some metaphors are created in precisely the same way. This is not to say that there is no difference between Kvasir and Dionysus. Cult practices have added to the stature of Dionysus and complicated his character. Nevertheless, in essence, in origin, they are blood brothers, and the drinkfest was essential to their generation.

2)   The god in the flowerpot

Here is a cactus plant in a flowerpot; it is small, spine-
less, grayish, apparently inedible and hardly a thing of
beauty by any aesthetic standard. The botanist would
recognize it as *Lophophora williamsii.* The scientist engaged in pharmaceutical research might identify it as a
source of the drug called mescaline. Wyoming Indians
refer to it among themselves as "the medicine," using
that word in its double meaning as a cure for illness and
a source of supernatural power. The Tarahumara Indians
of Mexico call it *hikuli,* and the Aztecs called it *peyotl.*
To the white men who are familiar with it, the peyote
cactus is a plant containing an interesting assortment of
alkaloids in varying proportions. To the Indians who use

it in religious ceremonies it is often more than a "medicine," it is a god. The plant, which has a limited range in extremely arid, almost uninhabited country along the Mexican border, is the object of annual pilgrimages by the Tarahumaras, who must make a journey of several days on foot to collect it. Oklahoma and Wyoming Indians import the dried "button" or raise peyote in pots. Whenever possible it is eaten fresh, without preparation; the dried button may be powdered, pounded into paste or made into tea. The god, being rendered fit for eating, presides over the meeting where peyote is taken and "sends" the songs sung and the visions seen by the members who partake of this sacrament. The peyote cult is not based on a written or spoken Word, but on the experience of the members during the communion.

My hypothetical flowerpot might have contained any one of a dozen plants, for instance, the Texas mountain laurel whose seeds are known as "mescal beans," several varieties of Datura including the jimsonweed of the American Southwest, certain lianas of the South American forests, a kava (awa) plant from Polynesia, the soma of ancient India, the haoma of the Parsis, the coca of Peru, or Indian hemp—the source of marijuana and hashish. The opium poppy would probably not be out of place. Several species of hallucinogenic mushrooms belong in the list, or would belong if they could be induced to grow in pots. I have used the American peyote because it is perhaps the most thoroughly documented of all these plants, none of which is valued for its vitamins or caloric content. All are drug plants: they inebriate, soothe pain or function as mind-changers. Some of them are open doors to the otherworld, and as such they have religious uses. They are sacred plants, magic herbs or shrubs, magic carpets on which the spirit of the shaman can travel through time and space. Like shamanism, which has been described as a religious technique rather than a religion in itself, the magic plants are vehicles for a special kind of experience adaptable to the use of most religions that acknowledge an otherworld and permit its exploration.

If there were such a field as theo-botany, the study of these plants and their cults would be work for a theo-botanist. As it is, little has been published in the way of comparative studies, perhaps for the very good reason that the scholar who attempts such a study must step out of his own field into four or five others, and thereby risk his reputation. Laymen, therefore, who have no prestige to lose, burst in where scholars fear to tread, and here am I. My own interest is in the mythology of the drug plants, and my approach has been by way of mythology, a study as perilous to the scholar as theo-botany. The hazards have therefore seemed less and the facts, such as we have, reassuringly firm. My approach to the subject was inadvertent, almost accidental; my experience that of one who has been treading water interminably and feels solid ground beneath his feet at last. Half a dozen important mythological themes—the shaman's journey, the food of immortal life, the food of occult knowledge, the fate of the disembodied soul, the communication with the dead, plant-deities—all converge on this point: that is, on some actual food (usually a drug plant) ritually consumed, *not* symbolically but for the experience it confers. Most of these drug plants are what Aldous Huxley calls "mind-changers." The experience differs according to the drug or mixture of drugs and alcohol taken by the shaman, the initiate or the communicant whoever he may be. He may fall into a coma lasting for a day or more; he may be awake, but anesthetized; his mind and body may be stimulated to wakefulness and fatigue dispelled so that he can perform feats of endurance quite impossible without the assistance of the drug. He may experience color visions of varying intensity. Euphoria, quickened or dulled sensation, a displaced center of consciousness seemingly *outside* the body, a sense of enormously protracted time and extended space, and a feeling of weightlessness, of escape from the forces of gravity, are among the possible effects. Usually the communicant fasts for a day or longer before taking the peyote, soma, mushroom or extract of jimsonweed. One good reason for the fast is of course the quicker and more powerful action of the drug on an empty stomach.

Bearing these facts in mind, let us return to the peyote and its mythology. So far as I know there is only one peyote myth, although there are many variations on the single theme. Since the peyote tradition has moved outward from the very limited peyote-growing region, the myth has presumably been passed along with the dried plants and the ritual. The peyote myth tells how an Indian (or several Indians—number, age, sex and condition varying according to the particular version) is lost or wounded and left for dead in an uninhabited desert region. Starving, thirsty, at the end of his strength, he stumbles upon the peyote. A voice tells him to eat it. He eats it and feels his strength miraculously restored. His hunger and thirst are alleviated, and he is able to make his way back to his people, to whom he bears the word of a new god sent to heal their suffering. Usually the Indian hears a voice directing him to eat the plant, or sees a godlike form in the shape of an Indian brave standing where the plant stood; in some versions he is given instructions by Peyote himself on the proper performance of the peyote ritual. Peyote has been used to prolong the endurance of dancers, to alleviate pain, to produce visions, to give courage in warfare and generally as a means of healing and communion in the peyote cults.

There are several points of almost equal importance in this brief summary. One is that the first man to eat peyote was very likely on the verge of starvation in that arid region where the plant grows. It is so unpalatable in appearance, so difficult to chew and swallow, that only a ravenously hungry man would be likely to make the effort. The lack of food plants in the peyote-growing area makes this hypothesis still more plausible. Furthermore, if a hungry man were to eat the fresh peyote he would almost certainly have a startling experience similar to the one described in the myth. His strength would be restored in an apparently miraculous manner and he would probably have hallucinations of some sort—visual or auditory or both. The peyote ritual, which presumably took shape gradually, was later attributed to the personified peyote, a god who was said to have revealed himself in a vision.

If the reader supposes that I am using the myth to shed light on the origins of the peyote cult, he is mistaken; I am using the *Lophophora williamsii* and all we know about it to shed light on the myth. It should be obvious at once that if we lift the myth from its cultural context, and substitute the word "cactus" or even "plant of life" for the word "peyote," the tale might quickly find its way into collections of myths and folklore concerned with *imaginary* fruits, leaves, roots or stalks that are sought over the earth, guarded by dragons, used to inspire poets, to lend strength to the arm of the warrior or renew the youth of the immortal gods. Should we conclude, then, that the myth of peyote's discovery is one variant on an almost universal theme attributable to the almost universal sameness of the unconscious mind? Or is it possible that the plants in the other myths are not necessarily imaginary? Are they, perhaps, real plants in imaginary gardens? Perhaps their mythical uses are derived from their cult use, and extended by hyperbole until the plant itself becomes mythical in the songs and retold tales.

The soma-drink of the Hindus was made from a real plant upon which the soma cult rested just as the Plains Indian or Tarahumara peyote cult rests upon the peyote plant. The soma plant, pounded, soaked, and wrung out on a strainer, provided a drink that was inebriating even without fermentation. The soma was deified as the god Soma, who inspired seers and poets and fortified the warrior. The kava-drink of Polynesia was prepared in much the same way from the kava plant (*Piper methysticum*, "intoxicating pepper") and was used as a ritual drink, as a libation poured to the gods, and as a trance-inducing beverage for the soothsayers. Both these plants have heavenly counterparts that provide a tipple for the gods. In other words, they have a mythology, and a much more extensive mythology than that of the peyote plant. The jimsonweed, prepared by maceration and mixed with water in a ceremonial bowl, was formerly used by some California Indians during initiations, when the novice was expected to see visions and gain shamanistic power. It, too, has its mythology. The sacred mushrooms of Oaxaca are taken raw, on an empty stomach, like the fresh peyote. When the shaman has swallowed the mushroom, the mushroom-deity takes possession of his body and speaks with the shaman's lips. The shaman does not say whether the sick child will live or die; the *mushroom says*. Some Indians say of sacred plants used by their shaman, that the soul of an ancestor has entered the plant; it is he who takes possession of the shaman and speaks through his mouth. The oracle at Delphi chewed laurel leaves for the same effect; in a state of inebriation induced by a small amount of cyanide in the laurel, she surrendered to the god (in this case Apollo), who used her as his instrument. His will was made known through her utterances delivered in trance and interpreted by the attendant priests. The laurel was, of course, sacred to Apollo.

Apollo, like the Norse god Odin and most shamans of whatever race or sect, was associated with healing as well as divination or prophecy. The same plant that brings visions or otherworld experiences may alleviate pain. Even if it does not, the herbalist who knows the medicinal uses of healing herbs has the best opportunity to possess the occult knowledge conferred by hallucinogenic shrubs and fungi. There are plants used to ease the pain of childbirth and myths of magic plants used for the same purpose. There is a Peruvian tale, very like the peyote myth cited above, telling how men first discovered the use of the cinchona bark from which quinine is made. If we begin our inquiry into the possible reality of the "magic" plants figuring in mythology with a compendium of real plants and their real uses in medicine, divination and religion, the list is immensely long and inevitably immensely tangled because medicine, divination and religion are tangled. Medicine enters this complex not because primitive medicine was limited to faith healing, but because the shrubs and herbs used in treatment were also used in religious ceremonies.

The most obvious thread for the ambitious theobotanist to grasp would be the relation of drug plants and intoxicants to shamanism and its characteristic mythology of the disembodied soul. The greatest obstacle the student would encounter is a dearth of knowledge about the drugs used and their precise effects on the nervous system. We know enough about shaman mythology to make a beginning, and we have many eyewitness accounts of shaman performances; but all too often we are told simply that the shaman "takes something," without being told what he takes. This gap in the narrative can be explained in part by the shaman's reluctance to give away his secrets, and in part by the fact that early informants were inclined to regard the shaman's act as Satanism if they were Christians or sheer hocus-pocus if they were skeptics. The current anthropological tendency, so far as I can make out, is to study the shaman as a psychological or cultural phenomenon. Mircea Eliade in his book *Le Chamanisme* mentions the use of drug plants by many shamans, but seems to consider the drugs incidental to the tradition. The pattern, he implies, is already formed; the drug, when discovered, is adapted to the shaman's use. This assumption parallels that of the mythologists who put the desire for an afterlife and the belief in an imaginary nectar of immortality before the experience of actual plants and beverages used in the ceremonial communion with the gods or the ancestors. The food of occult knowledge, by the same token, is treated as fiction; and when the shaman drinks a mysterious beverage, it is assumed that he does so in pretense that it is the mythical draught. But isn't this putting Medea's chariot before her team of serpents?

When we consider the origin of the mythologies and cults related to drug plants, we should surely ask ourselves which, after all, was more likely to happen first: the spontaneously generated idea of an afterlife in which the disembodied soul, liberated from the restrictions of time and space, experiences eternal bliss, or the accidental discovery of hallucinogenic plants that give a sense of euphoria, dislocate the center of consciousness, and distort time and space, making them balloon outward in greatly expanded vistas? A belief in the soul's reincarnation would seem to me more plausible than the widespread idea of a soul's continued independent, disincarnate existence after it leaves the body, a concept usually explained by night-dreaming or an irrational fear of the dead. Perhaps the old theories are right, but we have to remember that the drug plants were there, waiting to give men a new idea based on a new experience. The experience might have had, I should think, an almost explosive effect on the largely dormant minds of men, causing them to think of things they had never thought of before. This, if you like, is direct revelation.

Trance, self-induced by whatever means, is an inseparable part of shamanism. During the trance the shaman's body is said to be emptied of his soul. There are two traditional interpretations of this phenomenon: one is the replacement of the shaman's soul by another spirit, that of a god, ancestor or deceased shaman. (The deceased shaman may of course be both god and ancestor, and any of the three may take animal form.) In the other interpretation, the one I am concerned with here, the liberated soul of the shaman goes on a journey, perhaps in search of a lost soul, perhaps as escort for the soul of one who has just died, conducting it to the land of the dead. The dislocated or liberated soul may fly across the pampa on a spirit-horse or ascend into the sky, to the moon or the North Star. R. G. Wasson, describing the effect of the divine mushroom taken in a séance at Huautla, says: "There is no better way to describe the

sensation than to say that it was as though my very soul
had been scooped out of my body and translated to a
point floating in space, leaving behind the husk of clay,
my body." This is the shaman's journey.

The effect of peyote or hallucinogenic mushrooms
taken ceremonially to the accompaniment of drums,
songs or the hypnotic chant of the shaman demanding
the descent of the spirit is naturally somewhat different
from that produced in a laboratory or office while a doc-
tor sits beside his subject with a notebook. Nevertheless,
Aldous Huxley's testimony on the effect of mescaline,
especially insofar as time is concerned, is eloquent: "I
could, of course, have looked at my watch," he says,
"but my watch, I knew, was in another universe. My
actual experience had been, was still, of an indefinite
duration or alternatively of a perpetual present made up
of one continually changing apocalypse." The mushrooms of Huautla do not contain mescaline, but the effect, according to Mr. Wasson, is similar: "The mushrooms sharpen, if anything, the sense of memory, while
they utterly destroy the sense of time. On the night that
we have described we lived through eons. When it
seemed to us that a sequence of visions had lasted for
years, our watches would tell us that only seconds had
passed." The Indians say of the mushrooms: *"Le llevan
ahí donde Dios está"*—"They carry you there where
God is."

When the soma is poured on straw, the souls of the
ancestors gather in their thousands to drink it, because
this is their food. When the kava is poured in libation or
drunk by the priests, the souls of the dead are invoked,
and the entry of the shaman into trance announces their
arrival. Ceremonially speaking, these are foods of disembodied spirits, but the Chinese have, in the Taoist

tradition, another variant of the food of immortality. Here the emphasis is not on shamanism or the consultation of oracles, but on mysticism combined with alchemy. The Taoists, in their search for an actual "food of immortality," experimented with drug plants and venoms. They knew the uses of laurel, Indian hemp and bufotenine extracted from the glands of the poisonous toad. They knew the *lingchih*, the "divine fungus" eaten by Taoist hermits and depicted by Taoist painters. In one of his poems, Li Po announces that he has swallowed the pellet of immortality "and before the lute's third playing"—that is, the third stanza of a song—"have achieved my element." Does anyone suppose that Li Po really believed that a pellet would make him immortal? Was his pellet simply imaginary? Or was he speaking of the euphoria conferred by one of the drug plants known to the Taoist priests? To me it seems clear that his pellet was as real as a pellet of peyote paste; it was to him a "food of life" in the same sense that our *aqua vitae* is a "water of life." I also suspect that at least half the other foods of life (apples, ambrosia, leaves, bark, roots and elixirs) had their beginnings in real plants. The "talking" grasses and trees that the shaman uses to bring on his trance are certainly real, and insofar as they are used by him for this purpose, they are foods of knowledge—that is, of occult knowledge. Looking at the matter coldly, unintoxicated and unentranced, I am willing to prophesy that fifty theo-botanists working for fifty years would make the current theories concerning the origins of much mythology and theology as out of date as pre-Copernican astronomy. I am the more willing to prophesy, since I am, alas, so unlikely to be proved wrong.

3) Moon mythology reconsidered

In all the welter of theory about myths, with its cross currents, riptides and winds that box the compass, the sun and moon, like the deified plants, offer a slight security. When sun and moon are personified and named under their own names, the myth is merged with fact and we have something to go on. Unfortunately the first scholars to take sun myths and moon myths as a starting point for their inquiries into mythology pushed their theories too far. They went on to see suns where there were no suns, and moons where there were no moons. Critics of the sun-and-moon school not only demonstrated the error but succeeded (perhaps unintentionally) in writing off sun myths and moon myths altogether.

The ridicule they heaped on their adversaries was so devastating that scholarly eyebrows still go up at mention of a moon myth. The folklorist Krappe, writing in the midst of the ensuing backwash, announced that the moon was of interest to primitive peoples only as an indicator of time and would not "in itself arouse anything like what we are pleased to call 'higher' feeling." At the same time, the evolutionary school of myth interpretation held that early religion was itself unrelated to "higher" feeling, having had its origin in fertility magic. The presence of the moon in mythology and religious symbolism could not be overlooked: the moon was clearly there, but these mythologists saw her only as a symbol of the forces of fertility, her waxing and waning being symbolic of the growth and decay of vegetation, her rhythms associated with the sexual rhythm of the human female, and so on. Interpreted in this fashion (still the prevailing fashion as I write) a moon myth is no longer a moon myth, but a fertility myth.

If we can disentangle ourselves from the controversies for a little, and contemplate the mythology itself, I think we are bound to come to the following conclusions: first, the nature mythologists were right in so far as there *are* moon myths and moon deities; second, Krappe was right when he said that the moon's chief importance was as an indicator of time; and third, the fertility school is right in so far as the farmer's mind is much on the success or failure of his crop, so that, if he has a moon deity, he is likely to pray to it to make the corn grow. Moon deities, however, seem to follow on ceremonies and festivals timed by the moon, not the other way around. These ceremonies are not necessarily inspired by an interest in agricultural magic, and may have no connection with it.

Moon-timed ceremonies have been explained as originating in a belief that there are critical times in the life of the moon, or in the circle of the year, just as there are in the lives of individuals—birth, puberty, marriage, and so on—and that the times of new and full moon, as well as the critical times in human life, demand the performance of rites. For instance, ceremonies performed at the dark of the moon are intended, according to this explanation, to assist the moon's reappearance. I find this difficult to believe. We must imagine the ceremony to have been instituted by a grown man or woman, not an infant, and any man or woman old enough to institute the ceremony must have known that the moon had been disappearing and reappearing regularly for years without any assistance from the dancers or medicine men. Dances are often performed at new and full moon, and foot races are run. Sometimes they are interpreted as helping the moon, sometimes not. The pertinent question is *when* would the dance be performed if not at full moon? Not on Saturday night, because there are no Saturday nights. Are they to be held only when all the dancers suddenly feel in the mood to dance? Only when the priest sees fit to announce them? Very few tribes, and still fewer towns, are satisfied to be so haphazard, and in the case of the more important festivals where people come from a distance, a set time is a great convenience. In most societies, a liturgical calendar has provided a framework for the ceremonial life of the people, and the moon has provided the calendar.

The lunar phases and movements may be used to time the New Year, the feast of the dead, the shaman ceremonies, perhaps initiation and periodic drinkfests. The months of pregnancy will be counted by the moon if they are counted at all. Marriages may be performed at full moon, or dark of the moon, or new moon. If the people live near a seacoast, the alliance between the movements of the moon and the movements of the sea will be noted, as well as the coincidence between the moon's movement and phases, and the life rhythms of shellfish and other sea creatures. A moon deity, therefore, may be characterized as a death god or death goddess, a midwife, a deity presiding over marriages, a deity of the sea and sea life. Almost any deity whose festival is timed by the lunar phases or the position of the moon in the sky may take on lunar characteristics. Shaman mythology and moon mythology are blended when the shaman times his performances by the moon, when he "dies" and returns to life after three days, like the moon, or when he flies to the moon on his soul-journey to the land of the dead. It is no wonder that the mythologist on the track of moon deities and moon myths is likely to find one wherever he turns.

If religion were simply a matter of individual belief, and mythology were a statement of that belief, there would be few moon myths and fewer moon deities. But in so far as people come together for ceremonials and merrymaking, in both of which they pay respects to their deities or the mythical founders of their society, there will be need for a designated time and place for people to meet. In so far as myths are connected with those occasions, the time and place of meeting may figure in the mythology. The place is the market square, dancing ground, temple, kiva, sacred grove, cave, stone circle, or perhaps the cemetery. The time is determined by the sun, moon and stars, and especially by the moon. Even the annual festival is most easily determined by the new moon or full moon that is nearest to a given star or constellation, as for instance, Aldebaran or the Pleiades.

I shall deal with these problems more fully in a later chapter. Here, perhaps it is enough to say that while some calendars, notably the ancient Egyptian and Central American, have a numerical rather than an astronomical framework, both retain elements obviously carried over from earlier lunar or lunisolar calendars. One of the oldest moon gods known is the Egyptian Thoth. He is usually portrayed with a human body and the head of a crane surmounted by horns and a lunar disk. Like many moon deities, he is not exclusively a representative of the moon; his lunar aspect is one of several and he is perhaps primarily a calendar deity. In one myth he even dices with the moon for part of her light. The light Thoth won was added to a former "year" of 360 days to make the solar year of 365 days, while the lunar year was diminished by five days to 355 (actually 354½). This is presumably a myth by any useful definition. The story can be traced back to a very early period in Egyptian history; but like many moon myths, it was invented deliberately by a man familiar with calendar problems, a man belonging to a society already well acquainted with the difficulties of keeping a calendar in harmony with the movements of the sun, moon and stars. Furthermore, the myth is a festival myth, because those five extra days were added to the year as birthdays for the five children of Nut, and were celebrated as a prolonged five-day New Year festival. Perhaps a laborer dragging stones into place for a pyramid believed that Isis, Osiris, Nephthys, Set and Horus actually were born on the five days when he celebrated their festivals. The calendar-maker could not possibly have believed it, because those days did not even exist until he ordered his calendar in the cycle of 360-plus-five days. The mythmaker did not believe his own tale, and I doubt that he expected his contemporaries to believe it. It was a good story, and was still being repeated more than two thousand years later to illustrate the discrepancy between the solar (tropical) year and the lunar year of twelve full moons.

Thoth as moon god was "reckoner of time" and "the Measurer," as well as Scribe of the Gods and the inventor of the exact sciences. The name of the Mesopotamian moon god (the Sumerian *Nanna*, the Semitic *Sin*) was expressed graphically by the number "30" combined with the sign for a deity. This god, according to the early god lists, was the originator of the calendrical sequence of days, months, and years. In Peru as in Egypt, although the sun god took precedence over the moon deity, the latter retained a hold on the festival calendar. The moon goddess was Mamaquilla, the wife of the sun god. She was a deity whose "functions were chiefly with reference to the calendar and the festivals and work connected therewith." Peruvian women in travail called upon Mamaquilla, as the Roman matron called on the moon goddess Lucina, the Greek on the moon goddess Artemis, or the White Goddess, Leukothea. So far as all these characteristics of the lunar mythomorph are concerned, I should like to emphasize that each of them rests upon prior intelligent application of observations of the moon; usually they also rest upon a religious use of the moon in so far as it provided a liturgical calendar.

The moon is visible from every part of the earth. Her position among the stars changes conspicuously from one night to the next, but to every man who observes her, from whatever vantage point on the earth's surface, the star that companions her on any given night in her journey across the sky will be the same star. As she

waxes and wanes, her rhythms are the same to every
moon-watcher. Every lunar calendar, therefore, is going
to resemble every other in some respects, whether the
two are of the same or independent origin. At the same
time, a lunar calendar is portable, and can go along as
cultural baggage with migrations of peoples to the
north, south, east or west. The period of human gesta-
tion is the same in all inhabited zones, and it is ordinarily
counted by moons. So far as associations between the
moon and the calendar, or the moon and midwifery, are
concerned, the coincidences we find in the mythology
are to be expected. As for the association between the
moon and the sea, we find it among people living near
the sea, but not among inland tribes who have never
encountered the sea. The association is based on observation of natural phenomena, not on the operations of
a creative unconscious.

The problems of coincidence in moon mythology
really begin with the widespread association of the moon
and immortality. Students of religion and folklore are
well acquainted with the moon as an intelligent creature
who knows the secret of resurrection after death. Eliade
says: "A mass of myths describe a 'message' given to
men by the moon through the intermediary of an animal (hare, dog, lizard or another) in which it promises
that 'as I die and rise to life again, so you shall also die
and rise to life again.' From either ignorance or ill will,
the messenger conveys the exact opposite, and declares
that man, unlike the moon, will never live again once
he is dead. This myth is extremely common in Africa,
but it is also found in Fiji, Australia, among the Ainus
and elsewhere."

Besides the "message" stories cited by Eliade, there
are other kinds of myths and many ceremonies con-

nected with the death and resurrection of the moon, some from Polynesia, some from the American Indians. Frazer says of them: "These stories which associated human immortality with the moon are products of a primitive philosophy which, meditating on the visible changes of the lunar orb, drew from the observation of its waxing and waning a dim notion that under a happier fate man might have been immortal like the moon, or rather that like it he might have undergone an endless cycle of death and resurrection, dying and then rising again from the dead after three days." The "primitive philosophy" of Frazer's theory has lost its respectability as an anthropological hypothesis; and Eliade's explanation that the moon is an archetypal symbol of "becoming" seems to me still less tenable. Let us look further.

There is another mythical theme that forms a double link between the moon and a belief in immortality. This is on the one hand the ceremonial food or drink which, although actual, is said to come from the moon, and, on the other, the mythical plants or elixirs of life or knowledge that are sometimes said to grow on the moon, sometimes identified with the moon deity. All three—the ceremonial drink, the mythical draught of the gods, and the moon personified—meet in the soma of the Hindus. The coincidences in this quarter are worth looking into for a clue to the whole problem of moon mythology and its origins. Take, for instance, the moon tree.

Briffault mentions a number of moon trees, palms for the most part, and explains them by the supposed influence of the moon on vegetation: the sap was said to rise and fall with the moon; the sap was therefore looked upon as the life blood or soul of the moon. "Accordingly the highest forms of divine inspiration are acquired by partaking of those lunar emanations, as by drinking the juice of the soma, or, in South America, the fermented concoction known as 'chicha' or other vegetable beverages . . . To chew the leaves or fibers of the lunar plant or shrub is the necessary preliminary to the acquisition of divine and prophetic inspiration."

The reader of the preceding chapters should be able to criticize this paragraph for himself. Palms, including those specifically mentioned by Briffault, are a source of palm wine, which is made from their sap. Palm wine is drunk not because it is believed to be an emanation of the moon, but because it is intoxicating and the drinkers like to be intoxicated. The only alcoholic beverage *not* made from vegetation is koumiss, made from mare's milk. The hundreds of drinks from fermented fruits and cereals are drunk for their intoxicating effect, not because, being vegetable in origin, they are believed to be lunar emanations. The shaman drinks his kava, soma, or toloache, not because he thinks he is drinking the soul of a deity, but because it furthers his efforts to bring on the trance state. As for chewing the leaves and bark of trees and bushes, the shrubs may be said to grow on the moon, but that is not why the prophet chews them. He chews them as the Mexican wise-woman chews the divine mushroom, as the Inca priest chewed the leaves of the coca plant, as the Delphic oracle chewed the laurel leaves sacred to Apollo—for the sake of the drug they contain. The question is, rather, why he names the moon as the source of his food of life or knowledge, and why he calls his sacred plant a moon tree.

The moon trees that give the shaman occult knowledge are paralleled, as I have indicated above, by ceremonial beverages and mythical elixirs prepared by,

grown on, or even identified with the moon. The Cora
Indians of Mexico drink a life-water supposed to come
from the moon; the pulque gods of the Aztecs wore the
lunar crescent in their ears; the Chinese Moon Rabbit is
pounding an elixir of life with his mortar and pestle.
Soma, the ceremonial drink of the Hindus, was actually
identified with the moon. Without losing his identity as
a personification of a ceremonial beverage prepared
from the soma plant, the deity Soma became a moon god
as well as a drink god. The full moon was described as
a bowl of soma drained by the gods and the ancestors:
that is, the moon itself was the draught of immortality.
Soma personified was married to the Nakshatras, the
divisions of the lunar calendar that established the
days of Hindu festivals. To the Hindus as to most other
peoples, the moon was chiefly important as an indicator
of time.

I cannot conceive that men were first inspired to
think of the possibility of personal immortality by observation of the moon's disappearance and reappearance, as Frazer suggested. It is much more important
that the belief in immortality goes hand in hand with
initiation rites or ceremonies in which the participants
commune with the gods or the ancestors. Ceremonial
drinking, or the taking of a drug plant of some sort, is
often a part of the initiation or communion. And in any
preliterate society well enough organized to have a
liturgical calendar, the ceremonies are usually timed by
the moon as they were in ancient India. The Christian
Easter, like the Jewish and Moslem festivals, is still
timed by the moon. The Far East is in the throes of
changing from moon-timed festivals to the Western
calendar, but the moon still keeps its hold on the popular folk festival. To people who spend most of their lives

in the open, and read time in the sky, the moon may almost be said to make a personal appearance during the ceremonies: then there are moon dances and moon drinks and mimed impersonations of the lunar deity. Given the moon, and an intoxicating ceremonial liquor, and a society orderly enough to decree special days and nights for its ceremonies, especially those that involve drinking or the use of a drug plant, the same kind of myth may be invented, or assembled from the same elements, time after time and in any part of the world. Then Soma will marry the Nakshatras; the pulque deities will wear the lunar crescent; the moon cow will give an intoxicating milk; the moon goddess will steal the nectar of immortality; the Moon Rabbit will acquire the mortar and pestle with which to prepare it; the moon will die and come to life again, and moon tree leaves will renew the youth of the angels. A branch of the moon tree carried by the soul will enable it to overcome the dangers of its difficult journey and reach heaven. The moon is seldom far from the mysteries that prepare the initiate for an afterlife, and may even be said to "teach" them. The message "lost" in the folktale is found in the myth.

PART II

4) The mythmaker as actor

Shamanism, which was the least of my interests when I began to study mythology, has become a principal theme in my interpretation of it largely because the shaman is an actor. Let me illustrate before I go on to discuss my reasons for thinking that this fact is of the first importance.

A creation story recorded among the Cahuilla Indians of California tells how two brothers hatched from two large eggs that appeared in the void. One brother, Mukat, began to create things and take them from his heart by way of his mouth. He created in this manner two insects, a lizard and a person. The brothers and the newly created creatures went on to try to get rid of the darkness which still prevailed, but as I read, I found myself pausing to ponder this extraordinary mode of creation. I had heard of creation from clay, creation by fiat, creation by parthenogenesis from either male or female, and all these seemed reasonable compared with the Cahuilla method. Finally I read on, and, having turned a few pages, came upon a description of a fiesta. The most important fiesta of the Cahuillas was an annual tribal mourning gathering. During the first three nights the creation story was sung in a queer, minor, chanting voice. The medicine men also performed tricks. Medicine men are much given to "magic" or sleight-of-hand performances, not only among the Cahuillas, but quite generally, and one of their favorite tricks is sword swallowing. Also, when the shaman heals by sucking, he often pretends to extract from the body of the patient a small toad or some insect which has been causing the illness. The Cahuilla medicine men combined these two tricks in one performance. They sang for a while, then shook with an even trembling all over, then thrust a stick down their throats and took an object from their hearts. The witness reported seeing a lizard produced in this manner. The trembling was said to be caused by the things that wanted to get out of the shaman's heart.

The performance in this case is obviously a dramatic version of the creation story; but, since we know that sword swallowing is a popular carnival trick and is practiced in other cultures without the creation story, we are justified in supposing that the sword-swallowing act inspired the story, and not the other way around. So far as I can find out, the Cahuilla mode of creation is unique in mythology. It is none the less a myth, like any other myth.

Science fiction is easy to account for: the maker sits

before a typewriter, or takes pen in hand, or dictates, but the story comes out of his head. It is deliberate artifice, and it comes to us in the pages of a book. The writer recognizes that he is writing fiction, and the reader accepts it as fiction. But myths, we assume, are invented as fact and accepted as fact because . . . well, why?

At this point most writing on mythology sticks in my throat as the shaman's wand would surely do if I tried to swallow it. Direct revelation by Satan himself has gone out of fashion as a respectable hypothesis. We no longer entertain the notion that early medicine men deliberately invented falsehoods and indoctrinated the populace. We do hold that palpably false tales, when they are myths, are believed implicitly even by their inventors. Only a psychologist could explain how this could happen, and the psychologists have done their best. They have postulated certain patterns of subconscious thought which emerge in ritual or narration; these are collectively thought and collectively believed.

If the reader has no difficulty with this explanation, he is well taken care of, and I am not writing for him. For my part, I hold that the origin of the myth given above lies not in symbolism or psychology, but in the action of the throat muscles. The act may have become a ritual through repetition, but it was performed originally to amaze and entertain, and seems to have had no association with sympathetic magic. The more credulous members of the audience no doubt believed what appeared to be the evidence of their own eyes; they believed that the shaman's heart created the lizard. Consequently they had no difficulty with the myth. But the chief factor in their belief was the vividness and eloquence of the performance.

Other acts performed by the shaman have a direct

bearing on mythology. The most significant of these is the narrated and mimed journey to the other world. The shaman's performance is especially notable in that it seems to be a spontaneous improvisation molded by a tradition. I cannot do better at this point than quote from Nora Chadwick writing on Tatar shamanism. After remarking that there are four elements in a shamanic performance—dance, music, poetry and dramatic or mimetic action—she says that all these "are combined by the shaman into a single artistic exhibition resembling a ballet. This ballet is invariably religious in character. Moreover the shaman himself is the sole or almost the sole performer, changing his voice mimetically to represent different persons, gods, or even animals; changing his actions and his dance at different stages in his religious progress to the spirit world; changing his music according to the scene and the milieu in which his spirit is sojourning, or in response to the mood and character of the various scenes through which in spirit he is conducting his hearers. The entire performance, while following a traditional outline, or a traditional channel of thought and traditional style, is nevertheless a more or less extempore performance."

Going into more detail, Czaplicka gives an account of a single performance among the Altaians of Siberia. This is much too long to quote entire, but here is a brief summary of a journey to the spirit land witnessed by a missionary named Chivalkoff, and recorded by Potanin. The *kam*, or shaman, has first to cross (in his song) the Altai mountains and the red sands of the Chinese desert. He crosses steppes of different colors, and an iron mountain. He breathes heavily as he surmounts difficult passes; he finds bones of shamans who have gone before him and failed. He comes to a sea bridged by a hair, and walks this with the greatest difficulty; he totters, almost falls, and recovers himself. Before the dwelling place of Erlik he is met by vicious dogs and appeases them with his gifts. He comes into the presence of the god, bows, declares who he is and why he has come. He is shouted at by the angry god, leaps back in terror, summons his courage and again advances. The *kam* then stoops and makes movements with his drum as though dipping wine, which he offers to Erlik. He "makes a shuddering movement like that of one who drinks strong wine," to indicate that Erlik has drunk. The god then grants requests and the *kam* returns in high spirits, flying on a goose.

Compare this with a performance from Sarawak (North Borneo) as given by Frazer. On this occasion two mediums together made the voyage to the land of the dead. They sat side by side on a small mat which was their boat. Each had a paddle. As they floated downstream, paddling all the while, they talked, "remarking on the swiftness of the stream, noticing the overhanging trees . . . and hurriedly warning each other of sunken rocks. Then came an upset; the two men, amid the excitement of the spectators, swam for their lives, splashing about real water which had been introduced into the room for the purpose. However, they succeeded in righting the bark, and resumed the voyage with nothing worse than a wetting. At last they landed in the underworld. Then the tenor of their conversation changed. They now remarked on the departed spirits whom they recognized and some of whom they accosted. 'There goes So-and-So,' they would say, 'as lame as ever' . . . and from time to time they would grasp at some imaginary object in the air and exhibit a little tobacco or sireh leaf to the wondering and credulous onlookers.

After about half an hour of this pantomime they dropped on their knees and went groping about the room, clutching at various things, till one of them announced that he had caught the soul they were looking for."

Another similar description comes from the Duwamish Indians of our North Pacific Coast. In the Spirit Canoe ceremony as witnessed by Haeberlin the shamans of the tribe mimed their journey to the land of the dead. Two rivers had to be crossed. The first was spanned by a fallen tree—a medicine pole laid on the ground. The shamans walked their poles very carefully so as not to slip off. If one slipped, the others had to carry him. They crossed the second river by canoe, using their magical poles as paddles, and so on.

Or for a quite different example involving possession by a well-known spirit, consider this account by Elliott of a performance by a Chinese *wu*-woman. "In Singapore, Kuan Yin is invariably the *shen* who is called upon by soul raisers to lead them into the kingdom of hell to seek out the souls of the dead. . . . After a few minutes the soul raiser's body begins to tremble, at first gently and then more violently. Her muttering becomes louder, and changes to a singsong chant. This is Kuan Yin speaking and asking what is required of her. The soul raiser reverts to her normal voice and asks that an audience be granted with a person in hell. Here she gives the name and date of death. Kuan Yin agrees and passes the request on to the keeper of hell. She is allowed through and passes into a land where there are many suffering souls. As she goes up a hill, she is assailed on all sides by souls who demand to be put in touch with their relatives in the land of the living." The medium

describes hell in its most gruesome aspects to an en-
thralled circle of listeners.

Behind all these dramatizations of a journey to the
spirit land there is, obviously, a belief in the continued
life of the soul after death. There is also a belief in the
possibility of communication with the souls of the dead
through the shaman. All the details of the soul's where-
abouts and the conditions under which it survives form
the mythology of immortality, as distinct from a belief
in immortality. In the dramatizations just described one
can see taking place the otherwise obscure process that
presents the toughest problem to the student who would
like to understand these matters rationally: the process
by which an imaginative creation is, so to speak, col-
lectivized. Each shaman is free to add details which
were not there before. As he adds them, he *acts* them,
and the audience participating receives the new shading
of the theme as part of its own mythology.

In cultures where we have no such dramatizations as
I have described, or at least no descriptions of miming,
we have shaman songs describing the same sort of
action. The shaman songs of the Miaos, a non-Chinese
people of south central China, are superb examples. The
shaman accompanies the soul to the spirit land after
death, step by step, encouraging it in the dangerous
journey:

> *You climb higher and higher up the mountain,*
> *The mountain top is very cold.*
> *The stone dragon opens his mouth wide.*
> *The stone tiger opens his mouth opposite.*
> *You must not fear. The priest carries his sword*
> *under his arm and is your companion.*

*Take a handful of hemp and push it into the stone
dragon's mouth. . . .*

This continues for many stanzas. The songs may be compared with the shaman songs of China surviving from
the Han period, and even (by way of certain Siberian
shamans who mime their ascent through the nine circles
of the heavens) with the Book of Enoch, the *Apocalypsis
Goliae,* or the *Divine Comedy* itself, wherein Virgil and
Beatrice are the guides.

Besides the soul journey there are other dramatizations connected with shamanism. Sometimes, especially
in initiations but also in other performances, the shaman
mimes his own death and return to life. He may do this
with the aid of a drug that induces narcosis. Eskimo
shamans have been known to stage a "murder" with
copious bloodletting, from which they arose with whole
skins. In other forms of dramatization the shaman is
possessed by a god or spirit, sometimes a spirit of the
opposite sex, the female shaman speaking with a male
voice and moving with a man's gestures, or the male
taking on the personality of the female. Sometimes the
shaman, being possessed by an animal spirit, makes animal noises and movements. Sometimes props are involved, as when a female shaman, by sticking fangs
under her lip, "becomes" a wolf—that is, she is possessed
by a wolf spirit. In other societies, among the Tlingit
Indians for example, the shaman wears one after another
the carved masks of animals and birds indicating successive possession by those spirits. The animal spirits are
not just any animal, but a specific animal god with
human characteristics like Raven and Coyote. One of
the most popular *shen* operating among the mediums of
Singapore is Monkey, who is also the hero of a Chinese

classic novel, well known in English through Arthur Waley's translation.

My contention here is that the dramatizations have influenced the mythology fully as much as the mythology has influenced the miming. If the male shaman speaks as a male human being without props, without masks or costume, without conveying a dramatic personality different from his own, he must be much less impressive than the shaman who undergoes a bold transformation. It behooves him to be inventive.

Of course there are, besides, other forms of religious dramatization, but most of them appear to be closely related to shamanism. In initiations, for instance, a journey approximating that of the shaman to the other world may be performed by all the boys in the tribe, through dances or ordeals. The labyrinth dance of Malekula seems to be a dramatization of a death journey. Ceremonies of initiation into secret societies follow the same pattern; and the secret societies themselves may develop into dramatic societies like those of the South Seas. The trance dances of Bali with their masks of witch and dragon are another example of miming within a tradition that yet allows for extemporization of details.

These traditions will bear comparison with the Italian *commedia dell'arte*. There, too, we have stock characters standing in a definite relationship to each other. These characters are mimed in a plot with a traditional theme and extemporized detail. They are recognized with joy by the audience, yet the introduction of novelty into the plot also pleases. New combinations can be formed, and even, in time, characters may change emphasis so that the clown becomes a villain or the victim becomes a tyrant. Performances of this sort, whether religious or not, take place especially at festival seasons. Punch and

Judy and Harlequin are close to the characters of mythology in so far as they are neither historical nor fictional in the sense that Julius Caesar is historical and Mr. Micawber is fictional. Let either Caesar or Mr. Micawber turn up in a Christmas pantomime year after year and he will begin to take on the mythological nature of a Harlequin or a Hercules, a St. George or a Tammuz.

I should certainly not wish to suggest that *all* myths take their start in play acting; however, I think it not improbable that a great majority of all narratives on the Orpheus theme have originated in the mimed journey of the shaman. The well known folk-tale motif of the sky-journey is most plausibly accounted for by reference to the shaman's or the soul's journey to the spirit land; and even the Swan Maiden who, as Joseph Campbell has pointed out, appears wherever shamanism is practiced, may be a memory of the dramatized flight of a shamaness, with or without a feather mantle. The familiar character of the psychopompus takes on energy and a third dimension when seen in the light of the shaman's performance. The mythology of the dying god should be related not only to agriculture and the ritual sacrifice of kings, but to the mimed death and return to life of the shaman. The mythology of animal gods, too, has surely been strongly influenced by the shaman's animal roles. Transformations of all kinds are commonplaces alike in mythology and shamanism.

In his essay "The Structural Study of Myth," Claude Levi-Strauss lays stress on the fact that a myth is not a poem. A poem, he says, cannot be translated without serious distortions because the words themselves are of the utmost importance, but a myth is a myth in any language. When the words of a myth are the words of

Aeschylus or Dante, they *are* important. However, it is true that myths are often highly visual, as if they were, indeed, an account of a dramatic action or a ballet. My own view is that a myth is not a poem unless it is clothed in words by a poet. It may, however, be a mime accompanied by a ὁ μῦθος, the spoken word.

5) To make the gods laugh

The study of mythology might be compared to the investigation of a sealed box. We do not know which is top or bottom, who sent it or why. It is a kind of Pandora's box in which one may hear the buzzing of malignant superstitions, or the voice of a universal religion, or, again, the heartbeat of a social organism. Some say the box is empty; if we hear anything, it is the sound of blood in our own ears, like the distant surf audible in a seashell. As for me, whenever I poke or shake that mysterious package I hear the sound of laughter. I hear other noises as well, but the laughter is unmistakable, completely spontaneous and usually ribald. There are times when I detect (I think) the very birth cry of Comedy.

When and where *was* Thalia born? The question appears to be unanswerable simply because she is so old. The paleoethnologist deals in bones and stones, but laughter is neither; the spade that opens the graves of prehistoric men will never strike on its fragments. Burials in this, that, or the other position may possibly indicate something about a man's religious belief, but they tell us nothing about his sense of humor. Lack of evidence, however, is no proof that human beings couldn't laugh at least as soon as they could talk. When I find authors who are willing to hazard guesses about the character and accomplishments of Early Man, about his fears of the dark or the dead, his practice of fertility magic and the probable beginnings of his social organization, I wonder why I find nothing about the existence or development of his sense of comedy. Are risibilities considered too sophisticated for our stone-age ancestors? I confess I haven't read *all* the books, but so far as I have got, very few writers seem to give the question a thought. Where was the funny man? Didn't some joker cut capers just for fun, to show off, or to get a laugh out of his drinking companions? If not, how unlike us our ancestors were.

Comedy began sometime, and a search for its possible beginnings will take us back at least as far as the art of the last Ice Age. There is in the "Devil's Oven," in the French valley of the Dordogne, a famous engraving of an upright figure apparently dancing and playing a rudimentary stringed instrument. The dancing legs and feet are human, the rest of the body is bovine with curved horns rearing above the head. According to our lights, we see in this figure the ubiquitous Horned God of hunters and cattle breeders, a mythical animal ancestor, a masked Cro-Magnon man making fertility magic, or a prehistoric clown. It is even possible to see all of them at once.

Religion, myths, and magic could have been already in existence when the artist was at work some 18,000 years ago, but we have no proof in his engraving or others like it. A child, familiar with Halloween masking but ignorant of anthropological lore, would probably see in these capering beast-men nothing more remarkable than people dressed up in furry skins and horns. Furthermore, the child who had never heard of magic rites would not wonder *why* inhabitants of the Dordogne valley disguised themselves in animal pelts and pranced about; he would assume that they were having fun.

The child is not aware that his own Halloween fun is a debased form of ancient ritual presumably harking back to pagan times and beyond. The disciple of Frazer, or the student influenced even at second and third hand by *The Golden Bough,* compares the Halloween masking to similar play of a religious nature in ancient times and "primitive" societies. No matter how far back he goes, the ultimate origin of the tradition still eludes him, but there is implicit in his hypothesis an evolution or scheme of development leading from a belief formed in the "muzzy mind of primitive man" (Frazer's words) to an act intended to have a supernatural effect—that is, to a ritual—and finally to the same act devoid of meaning, a mere game for children. We have no proof, however, that the tradition has not come full circle. An act capable of giving fun to children now was probably fun to our remote ancestors before any beliefs became attached to it. The Cro-Magnon mind may well have been more childlike than muzzy. Even if the engraving in the "Devil's Oven" does represent a sorcerer, the sorcerer represented can hardly have been the first man to dress up in, say, a goatskin, and bleat: "Look at me—I'm a goat!" My argument for the primary impulse to don an animal disguise still stands. All that is needed is a pelt in a more or less intact condition, and an instinct, not for religion or magic, but for clowning. One of my many quarrels with Sir James Frazer hinges on his seeming inability to imagine that any act associated with religion could have been performed in the first place simply because it was fun.

Take, for instance, dancing and drinking. Both have their religious uses. Fermented beverages, as I have already pointed out, can only have been discovered accidentally. The various methods of brewing were surely devised because men liked to drink, and the brew was afterwards adapted to ceremonial uses, sometimes even restricted to ceremonial use. When the whole tribe drinks to a point of stupefaction on New Year's Eve, religious reasons may be given for the debauch, but they should not delude us into thinking that all the drinkers are drinking out of a sense of duty, to make magic. Most of them are drinking for the same reason people have always drunk. Their tradition only tells them *when* to get drunk.

The sacred beverages have had less attention than the sacred dances, but even ritual dancing is usually studied with an eye to its presumed magical effect rather than observed as an activity that may arise out of simple delight in rhythmic movement. Curt Sachs, in his history of the dance, says that some peoples seem to take no pleasure in dancing. They are not inventive, and they dance their traditional dances doggedly, at the prescribed season, because tradition says they must. Others obviously enjoy dancing. Their dances are full of mimicry, especially of animals, and they like to invent new

dances. Nobody knows, of course, whether the first lot
lost an earlier spontaneity, or whether the second developed inventiveness, or whether they were tempera-
mentally different from the Creation. However, I cannot
conceive of a man who danced only out of a sense of
obligation actually inventing a first dance. We should
have to suppose that he somehow reasoned his way into
the notion that jumping up and down would make the
corn grow. Therefore he jumped up and down, and so
invented dancing. I don't suppose for a moment that
people reasoned their way into dancing, drinking, or
mummery of the sort we see on Halloween. They performed all three acts for the fun of it, and afterwards
supplied the reasons, religious or secular, for continu-
ing what had already become a custom. A world-wide
comparison of similar acts accompanied by similar reasons for the performance will show, of course, a striking
similarity; on the other hand a world-wide comparison of
similar—in fact almost identical—acts, each with a different reason given for the action, will show a remarkable diversity. Frazer made the former comparison, laying stress on the reason or belief which, by implication
at least, precedes the performance of the act. But no
belief in the magical efficacy of drunkenness is really
needed to explain the phenomenon, which must in fact
precede the belief.

To the anthropologist, if I have any among my readers, I shall seem to be flogging a dead horse when I take
issue with Frazer. However, Frazer is still an authority
to be reckoned with in the literary world. We continue
to fall back on him partly because we lack another
equally available and extensive reference work on mythology, partly because of his influence, whether directly
or by way of Harrison and Weston, on such influential

moderns as T. S. Eliot. When one's field is literature, one can't get around *The Golden Bough;* one must go through it, or take it in some predigested form. The result is that nine out of ten of my readers have probably derived their notions about festivals from that work. As usual, Frazer's emphasis is on the intention which, he assumes, precedes and gives rise to the festival.

Now festivals have their uses, quite aside from any magical intention. They cut a pattern in time, break the monotony and relieve the boredom of day-in-and-day-out existence. They serve as a focal point in time much as the temple and market place serve as focal points in space for the life of the community. Festivals are something to anticipate and remember. They indicate a proper day for performing certain duties which might otherwise be left undone. They generate a sense of solidarity, an emotional oneness in the life of unsophisticated societies, and even, at times, in ours. They provide an occasion for dressing up, dancing, drinking, and going visiting. Children like them; simple people like them. Festivals in short are fun, and obligations be hanged.

Festivals, however, can be costumed much as dances are costumed. They are given a story line. Winter solstice festivals, for instance, are "intended" to make the sun turn round, although a winter solstice festival would be impossible to a people who did not already know that the sun turned round, and *when* it turned round, festival or no festival. So, dancers dance to make the corn grow, and drinkers drink to make rain. Festivals also give an opportunity for dramatic performances, when the gods may make an appearance by taking possession of their impersonators. The entertainments involving the appearance of the gods are among the most popular of all festival traditions. Whether the gods were already hanging about in the wings, waiting for the festival to take place in order to show themselves; whether they were generated by festival conditions— rich, god-producing soil—nobody knows. I should think that there must have been a constant interplay of per- sonification, impersonation, dramatization, until the di- vine mythomorph and the myth itself took shape. Even the presence of the gods does not mean that all the fun has gone out of the festival. The gods themselves are capable of laughter, capable of provoking laughter, and, if we are to judge by their myths, their sense of humor was not remarkable for its delicacy.

The Homeric gods roared with laughter at the lame smith-god Hephaistos mimicking graceful Hebe, and they laughed again when Aphrodite and her lover were entangled in a net forged by the outraged husband. The Japanese gods shook the heavens with their laughter when the goddess Uzume, lightly clad in moss and vine tendrils, performed a strip-dance on a drum. The grief- stricken Demeter laughed when Baubo exposed her nakedness; and when the Egyptian god Re had a fit of the sulks, Hathor made him laugh with the same gesture. The *Prose Edda* tells us that when Skadi armed herself and went to war against the Norse gods, she would agree to a truce on only two conditions, one of which was that they should make her laugh, "a thing she thought they would not be able to accomplish. . . . Then Loki did this: he tied a cord to the beard of a goat, the other end being about his own genitals, and each gave way in turn, and each of the two screeched loudly; then Loki let himself fall onto Skadi's knee, and she laughed."

Loki has been compared, with reason, to the trickster god of the American Indians. This comic mythomorph

can be studied in a little book of stories collected by
Paul Radin. The stories themselves are rather tedious,
at least on the page, though they are said to make the
Winnebagos roll with laughter. The most interesting
parts of the book to me are the prefatory note by Radin
and the commentaries by Jung and Kerenyi. Their notes
are as remarkable for what they leave unsaid as for what
they actually say.

The Trickster, like the clown or court fool, is both
cunning and foolish. His sexuality is exaggerated, another comic trait. Like Loki, the American trickster god
is a shape changer, often found in animal form. To some
tribes he is Coyote, to some Raven, to some the Master
Rabbit or Great Hare, yet he is always more human
than animal, and sometimes he is more divine than
human. In the Raven stories he is the creator.

Kerenyi, after a brief description of the Trickster,
asks: "How are we to conceive that unrecorded original
situation in which a story is told about him for the first
time?" The story, he goes on to say, must have dealt
"with a figure clearly envisaged by the eye of the mythmaker." And again: "Suddenly he must have sprung
forth, the trickster behind all tricksters, and have been
there so compellingly that all who heard tell of him
recognized him at once as the figure whom the story-
teller had in mind." Kerenyi is obviously sketching an
archetype that dwells in the collective unconscious; I
should find the spontaneous recognition more plausible
if the first audience were already acquainted with the
trickster as a clown, foolish-drunk, cavorting, and leading the revels in an animal mask. In the same volume
Paul Radin points out that the Trickster is found among
the simplest aboriginal tribes and in complex societies.
"Many of the Trickster's traits," he writes, "were per-

petuated in the figure of the medieval jester, and have survived right up to the present day in the Punch-and-Judy plays and in the clown." Is there any reason to suppose that the clown did not exist *as a clown* even before those archaic times when the mythical trickster first appeared fully developed in a tale? In order to tell a story, a man must at least have language, but a clown need not speak. His best medium of communication is pantomime. With or without his animal get-up, all he needs is an impulse to mimicry, an impulse to make fun, to make-believe, and to make people laugh. The buffoon could be as old as the human race, although we need not go that far to make him older than any myth.

Mere distance in time is still not enough to eliminate the difference between a clown as we think of a clown and a god as we think of a god. As Jung points out, however, the shaman who acts out his possession by a god or an animal spirit is not far removed from the clown. The most striking synthesis is in the mythology of Raven, where creator, shaman, and Trickster plainly meet. The shaman, as we have seen, is an entertainer in societies where his séances offer the only dramatic diversion: he is juggler, sword-swallower, an adept at ventriloquism and sleight-of-hand tricks. He changes sex. He dies and comes to life again; he flies to the moon. These are not narratives, but theatrical performances, like the performance of the clown or buffoon. The association between clown and shaman is clearer than the reason for the association. Is the unconscious or preconscious archetypal Trickster projected in the shaman's role as Dr. Jung seems to think? Or has the shaman helped himself to some of the clown's tricks simply because they are effective? Or did a god take possession of the clown and turn him into a shaman? Whatever the answer, my impression is that the Trickster holds a central position in mythology only in shaman societies—that is, in those societies where shamanism is the principal form of religious expression. In more elaborate religious systems, more complex and, especially, more literate societies, the Trickster often seems an interloper; it is he who interrupts the feast of the gods, or steals the food of life (like Loki or the Hindu eclipse-monster, Rahu). Sometimes he clings like a grotesque shadow to the heels of a god or hero, as the perplexing shape of a buffoon dances at the heels of the Greek Hercules. Sometimes he is a demon; the devil himself, with his animal hoofs, horns, and tail, is a comic character in medieval drama.

Another figure that helps to bridge the gap between god and fun maker is the leader of the revels, whether god, man or devil. Is Bacchus, in his leopard skin, with vine leaves in his hair, a personification of the power of the vine, or is he a masked Rex of some pagan Mardi Gras who has undergone apotheosis? We do know that the man who is intoxicated by a sacred drink or plant is often said to be possessed by a god; for the time being he *is* the god, in a temporary apotheosis. Perhaps, then, Bacchus is both the reveller and the intoxicant. The most plausible answer to questions of theogenesis probably lies always in the interplay of act and fancy. It is impossible that any society could have invented its revels, with drinking, dancing, masking and horseplay, to honor an *already existing* god of the revels. Greek comedy apparently grew out of the Greek revel (komos), and the revels followed upon the invention of the wine that intoxicated the dancers. Bacchus, "that first from out the purple grape / Crushed the sweet poison of misused wine," presided over the merrymaking.

Of course it is possible to revel without wine, but the

wine is a natural accompaniment. Again, no one knows how long human beings have been brewing intoxicating liquors or using, with or without religious reverence, drug plants that intoxicate without fermentation. One may at least point to a suggestive piece of sculpture sometimes called the Venus of Laussel. It is roughly contemporary with the Ice Age engravings mentioned earlier, and it shows a naked woman with her left hand on her belly, and a horn, apparently a drinking horn, held aloft in the right. The drinking horn may have contained spring water, but I doubt it. This female has been labeled a fertility goddess on no very certain grounds. She might as well be the first version of the Maenad or a Comus in female form. If the horn contained mead, the mead may have been regarded as sacred. On the information we have, we cannot possibly say whether or not the sculpture has a religious connotation.

Perhaps men conceived their gods long before they discovered drinking; perhaps they initiated religious rites before they invented horseplay. This last is difficult for me to believe, but I am willing to grant the "perhaps" since we can never know. Nevertheless, at some very remote time in our history, we did begin to laugh, we did begin to drink, dance, and parade in masks for the fun of it. Activity of the sort Enid Welsford calls "revel" as distinguished from "ritual" is attached like ritual to festivals. Perhaps, as she suggests, revel sometimes hardens into ritual, or ritual dissolves in revel, but the revel is there originally simply for its own sake. It can precede ritual; it can outlive ritual, and it has had as much influence on the creation of myths as ritual has ever had. If we ignore the spontaneous laughter, the fun that people find in festivals, the prankster whose only motive is to make people laugh, we are in danger of misreading mythology and miswriting history. Comedy may have held the stage before Tragedy arrived; surely the clown was making his brothers laugh before he attempted to amuse the gods.

6) A dragon hunt

The dragon, like the guest speaker at a banquet, needs
no introduction. Everyone has had some previous acquaintance with dragons in fairy tales, hagiology, opera,
painting and sculpture, or festival pageantry. Dragons
cause eclipses by swallowing the moon; they are vanquished by gods, kings, or heroes; they are made drunk
on mead or tamed with holy water; they bring good
luck at the New Year. The dragon's one unchanging
characteristic is his reptilian or serpentine body. He is a
monstrous, snakelike creature, ubiquitous and nonexistent. He may be feathered, horned or fiery, male or
female, evil or benign.

Some eager students of mythology and folklore have

hunted the dragon around the world in the hope of finding the ancestor of all dragonkind in the East, West, or Middle East. Others have tried to find the genesis of the dragon in the symbolism of the Unconscious. Others see in him a memory of giant reptiles long since extinct. Anyone who makes a painstaking comparison of dragon myths will surely conclude as I have that, while some dragon plots have very likely been passed along or exchanged among neighboring peoples, the dragon as mythomorph has been invented repeatedly. Once invented, he easily takes his place among other mythological personae, gods and heroes, often as a contestant in an annual battle. As for his symbolism, that differs from one myth to another, and the effort to make all dragons emanate from one unconscious fear or desire is useless. Dragons have been described as symbolic of rain-bearing clouds, fire, drought, rivers, darkness, time, evil, the unknown, one's father, the *status quo,* the Milky Way, the heavenly movements, and other assorted phenomena. St. George's dragon is symbolic of heresy. The ancient Babylonian dragon Tiamat, a female who figured in the creation drama, is said to have been symbolic of chaos; at any rate she was subdued, bound, cut in half, and placed over and under the earth to form the heavens and the waters beneath the earth. The Maya dragon wears constellation symbols on his flank and pours flood water from his mouth. The pursuit of dragon symbolism is entertaining, but it gets us nowhere so far as the genesis of the dragon is concerned. We have to account first for the creature's existence, then turn to the great variety of vehicles—oxcarts, sleighs, gigs and triumphal chariots—to which he has been harnessed.

Where *is* the dragon? If a child asked us in the month of July, "Where is Santa Claus now?" and if we were determined to be done with this nonsense (which is the way I feel about dragons), we might take the little question-box up to the attic and show him a red padded suit and a set of false white whiskers laid away in mothballs waiting for next Christmas. Likewise, if we were to go to the nearest Chinatown and hunt down the dragon, we should find his rippling hide, his great painted and gilded head laid away in a storeroom, waiting for the Chinese New Year. When that day comes, he will be taken out and paraded through the streets, frisking on perhaps a hundred prancing feet in an animated serpentine dance. Except for his greater size, the Chinese dragon resembles almost exactly the dragon called La Tarasque, of Tarascon in southern France, whose reptilian body was animated by eleven gentlemen. A twelfth, who served as leader of the dance, wore the dragon head and worked the mechanical jaws and the snort. La Tarasque made her appearance in the streets twice annually, once at the Feast of Pentecost, and again on St. Martha's day, when a young girl impersonating the saint led her through the streets on a ribbon and tamed her obstreperous movements with a dash of holy water.

These are real dragons, or at any rate real versions of imaginary dragons. Usually, I believe, it is assumed that the festival dragon was invented as an impersonation or representation of an already familiar mythological dragon haunting the seas, skies, or forests. But is there any good reason for that assumption? Was the archetypal dragon first conceived in the imagination and later impersonated by dancers, or was he not, rather, invented by the serpentine dancers themselves when one of them suddenly cried: "Look, we're making a big snake!" I confess that the second hypothesis had never entered my head until I noticed the association of the dragon myth and the annual festival, especially that of the New Year, and the parallel association between the serpentine dance and the New Year celebration. In China, where the dragon is most at home, the two are one, and certainly a conga-line of naked dancers is nothing but a naked monster snake, that is, a naked dragon. Isn't this, then, a possible genesis of the dragon, an archetype first observed in the flesh and elaborated in the imagination?

If we ask which is older, the snake dance or the dragon, the answer is surely in favor of the dance. Kohler's observation of his apes improvising a follow-the-leader dance around a pole would indicate that this kind of play might well be older than speech. If the mind of the ape harbors dragon images we shall probably never find out about them. I doubt that it does. The snake dance, at any rate, must have been invented spontaneously in different ages and in different parts of the earth, and has continued as a popular dance to the present time. The round and the serpentine are the two simplest forms of social dancing; and the serpentine, perhaps because an unlimited number of dancers can take part in it, is the most popular of all carnival dances. Even in societies where caste distinctions are rather rigid and the sexes do not often share the same pastimes, the serpentine may be all inclusive.

Sahagun described Aztec dancers, men and women, chieftains and others, who formed "one single big snake" that danced until the sun went down. Other observers have spoken of dances that resembled gigantic centipedes. This is the logical descriptive metaphor that we use ourselves whenever we speak of a "serpentine" or "snake" dance. In England a procession of schoolchildren marching two-by-two is a "crocodile," broader and not so long, but having a head and a tail and an undulant, purposeful movement.

Anyone who has stood on a high point after dark, and watched a lighted train twisting through the valley below him, will agree that a fiery snake or worm is the image that immediately comes to mind. I have never had the experience, myself, of standing on a hillside at night to watch a serpentine torch dance on the plain below me, but surely such a dance would appear to the observer as a giant snake with fiery coils. I have never watched a snake dance in which the dancers wore feathered headdresses and cloaks, but, if I should see one, I imagine that it would put me in mind of a monstrous feathered serpent. When the first priest, sorcerer, or leader of the dance put on an animal mask with horns, the horned dragon appeared upon the face of the earth. When the animal-headed snake dance, coiling around a tree or funeral mound, joined head to tail in a round dance, the Midgard serpent was born. In northern mythology he encircled the earth; in the astrological tradition he became the symbol of Saturn.

The more I have considered the dragon as a mythomorph originating in the snake dance, the serpentine or spiral procession, the more the possibility has grown on me. If I am right, the dragon is animated as the snake dancers move, and takes his appearance, including his color, from their costume. The next question to ask ourselves is, What does the dragon do? Aside, that is, from swallowing his own tail?

First, dragons engage in duels. Throughout the East, Middle East and West, the dragon can be found in combat with another dragon or a hero. A mock battle is, again, a typical feature of folk festivals, especially at the New Year. The contest may be a tournament, a tug of war, a pantomime battle between two men costumed as lions, a wrestling match or other athletic competition, an archery contest, a sword dance, or even a Rose Bowl game. Sometimes the dancing dragon appears to be combined with a ritual or dramatic combat, at least in the myths, and possibly in the annual performance of the myth as well. In real life there have been, we know, symbolic combats between the forces of summer and winter, costumed in white and red respectively. In a Celtic myth, instead of a conflict between dragon and hero, we have a battle between two dragons, one red, one white. Another pair of Celtic dragons who fought every May Day eve were overcome when they passed out after drinking too much mead, a likely enough end for festival dragons. They were then folded away in a chest and buried in a hillside. The Celtic pairs have a parallel in China where two dragons contend endlessly for their mysterious "pearl"—apparently the moon—in an ancient tradition. The Babylonian dragon called Tiamat (mentioned above) was conquered by Marduk in a New Year performance; and Illuyankas, another drunken dragon, was defeated by the chief god of the Hittites in another New Year drama. When the dragon's head is severed from its tail, the head sometimes fights on alone, a feat easily accomplished by dragon dancers.

Dragons are also guardians. Like festival dancers they are forever coiling around sacred trees or sacred wells. In Greek mythology we hear of a fiery dragon who guarded the sacred well at Thebes: in death he was metamorphosed into two bodies of armed men who fought each other until all were killed. Another tree-encircling dragon was guardian of the Golden Fleece; he was put to sleep by Jason with juices from Medea's herbs. A third Greek dragon, Ladon, guarded the tree of golden apples in the Hesperides, and now winds his sinuous length around the celestial pole as the constellation Draco. In the North there was Fafnir, guardian of the Rhinegold, whose blood on Sigurd's tongue gave understanding of the speech of birds. There are in Hindu mythology two giant serpents guarding the honey of eternal life in the Himalayas; and so it goes. The guardian becomes an antagonist when his treasure is threatened by the protagonist of the drama.

The mythological forests are full of dragons, so many that a tour of their lairs might weary my reader. In case he cares to go exploring on his own, let me recommend the Japanese eight-headed dragon made drunk on eight tubs of saké and dispatched by a sword drawn from his own tail, the same sword that still forms part of the Japanese imperial regalia. Then there is the Python, vanquished by Apollo, and the seven-headed Hydra killed by Hercules. St. Margaret was swallowed by a dragon whose sides burst open, allowing her to emerge unharmed, a legend paralleling the well-known mythology of the eclipse-dragon who swallows the moon or sun.

The eclipse-dragon is too complex to deal with here, since a proper discussion of eclipse myths involves both an astronomical knowledge of eclipses and a discussion of the swallowing-myths (like that of St. Margaret) in general. I shall only say that the man who had never heard of, or seen, or imagined a dragon elsewhere, could never have *seen* a dragon in either a solar or lunar eclipse. There are swallowing dances of the London Bridge type, as well as swallowing myths; the swallowing dance is related to the snake dance as the swallowing myth is related to the dragon myth. The reader who wishes to toy with the juxtaposition of these themes can easily find examples of both. I can warn him, however, that he will soon find himself following the twisted paths traveled by the souls of the dead through dragonlike labyrinths and spiraling labyrinthine dragons, some choreographic, some architectural. Eventually the dragon's jaws become the Jaws of Hell itself. Good luck to the adventurer. Others have gone that way and returned, or so they say.

There are among all these dragon myths problems of relationship that will probably never be solved. Is the Hittite Illuyankas, for instance, a second cousin once-removed of Babylonian Tiamat? The overlapping mythological roles of serpents and dragons raise other questions. The naga of Hindu mythology is half serpent, half human, like Mélusine when she took her Saturday bath, or Lilith in Italian Renaissance painting. The Hindu eclipse-dragon is a naga with human head and cobra body, entirely unlike the Chinese dragon of the eclipse although their roles are identical. Certainly there have been borrowings; also snakes themselves account not only for snake mythology but for elements in dragon mythology. Snake symbolism is almost as varied as dragon symbolism, and it would be wonderful indeed if the two themes did not overlap. The dragon, however, is not a snake but a serpentine monster, large enough for a man to walk into his open jaws; he may be feathered, winged, horned, with a lionlike or wolflike head, with lion claws or bird talons. He is not a cobra, not a rattlesnake, not even a dinosaur. He (or she) performs at festivals, and plays an important part in festival mythology. Ubiquitous and yet unreal, the dragon is more at home in carnival plays and pantomime than it has ever been in theology, natural history, or abnormal psychology.

The origin I have suggested for the dragon would have two advantages: it would account both for the independent invention of the same (or virtually the same) mythomorph in widely separated and very diverse cultures, and at the same time it would account for the borrowing and lending of dragon plots wherever the "big snake" already existed, not as a symbol, but as a form of play.

PART III

7)   Who was Hathor?

If we ask, "Who was Clara Smith?" we shall receive a number of different answers depending on whom we ask and what that person knows of her as mother, daughter, schoolmate, grandmother, sister, neighbor or friend, yet she is bracketed between her birth and death dates, and she was never known to be in two places at the same time. In the case of a goddess the variety is multiplied, the life span is extended, the limitations of time and space no longer hold. She is here, there, and everywhere in a dozen guises, and all simultaneously; yet we believe that she is not and never was. How then can we say *who* she was?

In Hathor's case we may begin by saying that she was

an Egyptian deity worshiped in the valley of the Nile; that her remotest beginnings are among the mysteries of predynastic Egypt; and that her worship continued into the Christian era (the last great gateway to her temple at Dendera was completed in the time of the Roman emperors). With nearly three thousand years of continuous worship under the same name in the same part of the world, Hathor may be described as one of the longest-lived deities on record, and perhaps on that account one of the most confusing. She is at once Hathor of Dendera, Hathor of the Sinai Peninsula, the Lady of Byblos, the "goddess of all foreigners." On the east coast of Africa she was Mistress of the Land of Punt. She is wife to Horus here, wife to Ptah there, and again daughter of Horus or daughter of Re. She is a woman, a tree, a cow, a sistrum, a raging lioness, and the Egyptian equivalent of the Greek Aphrodite. She is goddess of the western hills. She is one, or seven. She has been described by modern writers as a Celestial Goddess, a universal abstract Mother Goddess, a Moon Goddess and an Earth Mother. She is also a goddess of the dead.

The only way to approach such a formidable deity is softly, step by step. If we never reach the inner shrine of the temple, we may at least establish order in the outer precincts. For a beginning, "when" and "where" are two of the first questions to ask about a deity, although we can seldom reply to them as we would reply to the same questions about a mortal. Rather, the answers will refer to when and where the deity receives worship, when and where her epiphanies take place. Ordinarily we can answer *where?* by naming a temple or temples, and *when?* by naming certain festivals. Religion has its personal aspects, but in its public form worship calls for a time and a place, either outdoors or indoors, for the gathering together of the worshipers.

Where Hathor is concerned we can at least answer that Dendera was the city of all cities most sacred to her from the earliest period down to the latest; she may even have originated as the local deity of that city. The temple that still stands there was built on the site of her earliest known place of worship. Her greatest festival was on New Year's Day, which was the anniversary of her birth. She seems to have shared the New Year festival with the sun god Re, and another festival, when she made a pilgrimage to Edfu, with the god Horus of that place.

Another question to ask is, "How was she worshiped?" Here the answer is unequivocal: Hathor "enjoyed immense popularity as the goddess of joy and love. She was proclaimed mistress of merriment and sovereign of the dance, mistress of music and sovereign of song, of leaping and jumping and the weaving of garlands. Her temple was the 'home of intoxication and a place of enjoyment.'" Her priestesses were beautiful dancing girls, and the columns of her temple were in the form of colossal sistrums, a kind of tinkling rattle used like a tambourine; the heads of the instruments were made in the likeness of Hathor's head. Although I find no reference saying in so many words that temple prostitution was practiced, the dancing girls seem to have been liberal with their favors. The Greeks translated Per-Hathor or "House of Hathor" as "Aphroditopolis."

Another pertinent question relates to the iconography of the deity. How is she depicted? In the first place she is a beautiful woman with horns on her head and a sun disk or moon disk between them. Since she has her birthday festival on New Year's Day, we might suspect that the horn and disk motif refers to her association with the calendar and the sun god Re. Whether she is entitled on this account to be known as a moon goddess is more dubious. Moon deities have certainly been portrayed wearing the horns of a cow, supposed to be symbols of the crescent moon. Hathor's association with the West, the quarter most often allotted to the moon, again hints at a lunar divinity, but the lunar aspect of Hathor was only one side of her personality, just as Hathor is at best only one aspect of the moon. Other deities, male and female, have shared the moon with her during the long course of Egypt's history. She is both more and less than the moon personified.

As a cow she may be the moon, but this, again, is only part of the cow symbolism. Perhaps she is a moon cow as she emerges from a papyrus thicket, but in another representation the pharaoh is kneeling to drink from her udder. Again she is a seated woman suckling the pharaoh or the infant Horus (she is his mother as well as his wife and daughter). A number of the scenes in which Hathor is giving suck to a human child have survived, but without a text to elucidate them. Is she still the moon, or are we now dealing with another aspect of the goddess?

As we continue our investigation, we find that the moon goddess and cow goddess have been blended with a tree goddess. Hathor is sometimes shown standing in a tree and pouring out a stream of the water of life; or, in other vignettes, she is the tree itself; one branch is a human arm and hand holding a pitcher from which the water of life is poured for souls of the dead to drink. As a goddess of the west she presides over the dead, but as a tree she also nourishes the dead just as she nourishes the pharaoh or the god Horus. The tree is either a sycamore (fig-mulberry) or date palm; presumably it stands in the other world. The souls come, sometimes in the form of birds, sometimes in human form, to drink the precious fluid it pours out. What have we here? A moon tree?

It is possible to maintain that once we start dealing with scenes of the afterlife nothing is reasonable, nothing is absurd, and we should not ask questions or seek answers. "They believed" thus and so, and that is enough. It is not enough for me. If the sycamore provides a fluid for which the dead thirst, I am convinced that it provides a drink, or some ingredient of a drink, that is also relished by the living. Wine is made from the date palm; wine may have been made from the fig-mulberry. We are told that Hathor's temple was the "home of intoxication," a state probably induced by some sort of ritual drink, either fermented or drugged. As we have seen in the case of Mayauel, the identification of a drink plant with a woman giving suck to a child is a perfectly natural one. In fact, Hathor is Mayauel all over again, even to the lunar associations. This need not mean a direct connection between Egypt and Mexico, but more likely a parallel development of the goddess as patroness of a divine drink. It is the one interpretation that binds the disparate fragments of Hathor's iconography together: the goddess whose "milk" feeds the divine child, the worshiper, and the souls of the dead; the goddess whose "milk" is drunk at the time of the new moon or full moon; the goddess whose "milk" intoxicates at the New Year.

There is a myth of Hathor that seems to me to confirm this interpretation. The myth is important for several reasons. In the first place, it is one of the oldest mythological texts in the world. It was inscribed on the four walls of a chamber in the cenotaph of Seti I, who lived about 1300 B.C. It is a New Year myth, directly related to the festival. The story is as follows:

Men were complaining that the sun god Re was growing old; they believed they should have a new god. Re called a conference of the oldest gods, and was advised to send out Hathor to punish the rebels and blasphemers. Hathor in the form of Sekhmet, "the Powerful," went forth as a raging lioness. She attacked furiously and found that she delighted in the kill. When Re called her to come home, she continued the carnage until she waded in blood to her hips. At last Re began to fear that all mankind would perish. He therefore ordered runners to go to Qeqt (near Aswan) for something called *tataat,* and at the same time caused seven thousand jugs of beer to be brewed. The *tataat* was mixed with beer to make a sleep-producing potion, which was red as blood. This was poured out in the fields where Hathor, mistaking it for blood, drank deeply of it and became too drunk to continue the slaughter. She returned peaceably to Re, who called her "beautiful one," and decreed that in the future "at every one of his festivals vessels of 'sleep-producing beer' should be made, and that their number should be the same as the number of handmaidens of Re." Budge says: "Those who took part in these festivals of Hathor and Re drank beer in very large quantities, and under the influence of the . . . priestesses, who were supposed to resemble Hathor in their physical attractions, the festal celebrations degenerated into drunken and licentious orgies."

This myth can be approached from more than one angle, and like most myths it shows a different face to each approach. Budge entitles it: "The Legend of the Destruction of Mankind." John A. Wilson, in *Ancient Near Eastern Texts,* uses the title: "Deliverance of Man-

kind from Destruction." In the latter volume the myth
is related only as far as the drunkenness of Hathor; a
note follows in parentheses: "(The remainder of this
story has to do with the origin of certain names and customs, such as the use of a strong but soporific drink at the
feast of Hathor.)" But isn't the use of a strong but
soporific drink at the New Year festival the whole point
of the story? The plot, as I read it, has to do not so much
with the rebellion and punishment of mankind as
with the blood-thirstiness and eventual pacification of
Hathor. My title would be "Hathor Drunk," and I should
compare it with the Hittite New Year myth of Illuyankas, a dragon overcome by liquor, rather than with flood
myths and the like. The case would be plainer, one way
or the other, if we only knew what the *tataat* (also
rendered *didi*) was or were. Budge assumes that the
tataat, as he calls it, was some soporific to be added to
the beer, and he tentatively accepts the suggestion,
made by Brugsch, that it was mandrake. Perhaps it was
poppy rather than mandragora. Some substance added
to beer apparently pacified the enraged Hathor and
gave pleasure at a New Year festival.

Whatever the *tataat* may have been, even if it was
only red coloring matter, this myth of Hathor raises certain questions that are to me most perplexing. Rudolf
Anthes writing in *Mythologies of the Ancient World*
says flatly: "Apparently the whole story is designed to
explain the custom of drinking to excess on the Feast
of Hathor." Or perhaps it explains the addition of a
soporific to the festival beer so that the celebrants would
not become belligerent after heavy drinking. In any
case, we have here what sounds like a deliberate invention, possibly by one of the priests at Dendera. The
myth resembles a scenario; the first act is the conference

of the gods in which the audience learns what the
trouble is and what the protagonist in the drama intends
to do about it. We shall probably never know whether
the myth of Hathor drunk was a kind of mystery play,
or whether the story was produced (perhaps to order?)
by a literate priest who wrote it out much as we have
it now. The perplexing question is: *If* he did, if the myth
had a single author who deliberately invented it and
wrote it down, either as a play or as a story, is it still
a myth? Did it come to be a myth only when it had been
handed down for several generations? Would it cease to
be a myth if we found the original version with the
author's name subscribed to it?

The same question might be asked of many myths, but
it seems especially pertinent to the story described
above. If a myth is usually, as we are told, a story of
gods and goddesses, this tale surely qualifies as a myth.
Hathor is indubitably a goddess. Myths are traditional;
the story of Hathor was current for centuries and may
be said to have become traditional, although it was not
traditional in the beginning. Nothing is. If a myth, as
some say, is a palpably untrue tale which is nevertheless
believed, we have to confess that we don't know who
believed the story; I doubt that its author believed it.
If a myth is a remembered rite, we have no evidence for
a rite corresponding to the tale, though we do have its
association with the custom of drinking to excess on the
New Year. If the story goes back long before Seti I, to
pre-Dynastic, preliterate times, *then*, presumably, it is
a myth.

But are we justified in considering it a myth on the
evidence in hand? My answer would be that it is a myth,
like most myths, by association: first, by association with
the goddess Hathor and second by association with a

festival custom. If our definition of a myth is not broad enough to include the story of Hathor, we shall find ourselves excluding most of the world's mythologies.

Hathor, then, is a cow, or cow-headed, a tree, a woman, but also in her bloodthirsty form a lioness, or a woman with the head of a lioness; in this guise she is known as Sekhmet, "the Powerful," and also as the Eye of Re. Even with these manifestations her variety is not exhausted since she is also represented in multiple form as several fairy godmothers appearing at the birth of a child to prophesy his destiny. Although these Fates are usually seven rather than three, they are occasionally nine or even twelve. They are depicted suckling the multiple souls of the infant, or beating their tambourines. Her collar or necklace called "Menat" had some mysterious significance for this life or the next; she is shown making a gift of it to Seti I. Her long hair divided into four locks is stretched to the cardinal points—"the symbol of the Archetypal Feminine as the world-governing totality in all its aspects," according to one author.

No matter what kind of boundary we try to draw around Hathor, she is likely to spill over it. We cannot describe her, or say who she was, in a single phrase, but it is possible to see a pattern that makes some sense out of the long worship accorded to her. Her only existence is in that worship, in dance and song and intoxication: that is "who" she is.

8) The soothsayers

The mythology of prophecy is a narrow corner of a very
broad field, yet, narrow as it is, a number of deities live
there. They are by some accounts among the oldest and
most powerful of the divine beings. The more I consider
them, the more convinced I am that divination, like
healing, has played a larger part in early religions than
we usually allot to it, and I think of it as arising in the
first place out of a simple desire to avoid making a decision.

We needn't quibble, I believe, over the mythmaker's
time sense or lack of it. Any man who works today on a
weapon he will use in tomorrow's hunt has a sense of
time to come. Faced with a decision—whether to go up-

stream or downstream in search of game, whether to go north or south to avoid the enemy—he may rely on reason to direct his choice, or he may, wavering between this and that, seize upon a chance omen: the flight of a bird or the pattern made by falling yarrow stalks. In the latter event he has taken the first step toward a mythology of the future. Although he is only asking, as Saul asked the ghost of the prophet Samuel, what he ought to do, not what is going to happen, the notion that the pattern of future time already exists is foreshadowed in the question.

From some seed such as this a system of forecasting events or determining courses of action may gradually develop; soon thereafter specialization probably sets in. Proper times for consulting auspices are established; certain people, either male or female, perform the ceremonies. These people usually wear a distinctive attire or carry some insignia of office. If a deity of divination takes shape, it is likely to take the shape of the diviner.

The shaman or seer, it is to be understood, serves not only individuals with personal problems, but like the Delphic oracle has an influence on public events. He (or she) is a member of the Establishment. In our society the gypsy fortune teller who reads the future in a pack of Tarot cards is virtually an outlaw. Under the circumstances, she could hardly become a goddess of destiny. But if instead of being barely tolerated by society she should become a support to it, then the face of Fate personified might well be a gypsy face between hoop earrings. This is the more plausible since gypsies, like the wise women of the past, are often believed to have the power of influencing through charms and spells the future that they foresee.

The weird sisters whom Macbeth encountered on the

heath are ambiguous creatures from popular mythology, wise women or witches with supernatural powers, of whom Holinshed says: "These women were either the weird sisters, that is the goddesses of destinie, or else some nimphs or feiries, endued with knowledge or prophecie by their Nicromanticall science." "To dree one's weird," as the reader is no doubt aware, means "to undergo one's destiny." The implication is that the weird sisters, like the Fates, not only foretold one's destiny but decreed it. However, even if they are goddesses of fate, they are envisioned in the form of the wise woman who makes fate known.

The "Nicromanticall science" Holinshed mentions is the art of revealing the future by communication with the spirits of the dead. The witch of Endor, who called up the ghost of Samuel, was a necromancer. The art is frequently practiced in connection with shamanism, since the ghost of the departed shaman may be called upon by his descendant or successor. The grave or tomb of a seer (like that of Mopsus in Greece) is frequently thought to be the proper place for a séance, and the powers of the dead shaman are sometimes believed to lodge in a fragment of the corpse, especially the skull or jawbone. In the Eddic poem *Voluspo*, the Norsemen's shaman god Odin calls upon a dead shamaness to reveal the future of the gods. Like many other seers, she begins by revealing how much she knows of the past, then goes on to divulge the Doom of the Gods. Wherever the dead are called upon as powers in the world of the living, they are only a step from godhood themselves. The euhemerist view that gods were originally living men is surely true to a limited extent in the case of the gods of shamanism. Richard Chase says, "The magical or terrible beasts, the witches and sorcerers, the tricksy or noble heroes of mythology should not be described as 'faded gods,' as they have sometimes been called; rather are the gods faded beasts, magicians, and heroes. Stated thus negatively, euhemerism is profoundly true." Another way of phrasing what I take to be the same idea would be to say: the shaman or seer casts an enlarged shadow having his own outline, and the shadow in the imagination of the audience becomes detached, capable of independent movement, and endowed with superior powers, similar to those attributed to the man. In short, it becomes a god.

On the distaff side we have not only Voluspo and the Weirds, but the Fatae or Parcae of the Romans, the Norns, and the Moirai of the Greeks. The triple form of these women poses an important and apparently insoluble problem. Has each set of three evolved independently of the others, and independently also of three-formed Hecate, the three swan-formed Graiai, the Brigit Triad, the Gorgons and the Celtic Deae Matrae? Or has the Mediterranean literary tradition spreading to the north caused one Norn to become three in imitation of the three Greek Fates, Clotho, Lachesis and Atropos? If they evolved independently, why are they triple? Are they, as Mr. Graves holds, three-formed because of an association with the moon, which is crescent, full and waning? Do they all represent past, present and future? Or are we to fall back on coincidence for an explanation?

An unknown mythmaker of preclassical antiquity may have invented the three Spinners and put them into a tale or song. The song (let us suppose) was handed about until the Spinners became familiar to a large audience and found their way into the mythology of northern Europe as three Norns, three Weirds or three fairy godmothers. On the other hand, the practice of divination by women may have led to the independent creation of the feminine deities of fate in different mythologies, and the triple form may be simply coincidence. Or, what is still more likely, female deities of destiny may have evolved independently as counterparts to the human practitioners of the Nicromanticall art and other branches of divination, their number being finally influenced by the literary tradition of the Parcae.

In the northern countries there is a significant association between the goddesses and certain human prototypes (as they appear to be). MacCulloch in *Eddic Mythology* explores this question at some length. He says: "Whatever the ultimate origin of the Norns and similar dispensers of destiny may have been, they had human counterparts in actual prophetesses or magic-wielders, like the old Scots 'spae-wife,' who foretold an infant's future, or the Norse Spakona or Volva. In some references to these it is not easy to say where the human aspect ends and the supernatural begins. As Grimm says, 'prophesying, inspiring and boon-bestowing women were always supposed to pass through the country, knocking at the houses of those whom they would bless,' and 'tales of traveling gifting sorceresses were much in vogue all through the Middle Ages.' In the story of Nornagest the Norns are called Volor and Spakonur, and are said to travel through the land. In Viga-Glumssaga a Volva or spae-wife called Oddibjorg goes about the land, prophesying and telling stories, her prophecies depending on the kind of entertainment which she receives. Quite possibly the supernatural Norns were a reflection of such actual women who claimed and were believed to possess powers of prophecy and even of influence on human destiny." The tradition of the three goddesses of fate survived into the Middle Ages in Brittany where places were laid with three knives for the fairy godmothers who were supposed to appear at the birth of a child or at the New Year.

In his book *The Great Mother* Erich Neumann writes of the female as muse and original seeress, who by "the consumption of intoxicants, the drinking of blood, poisoning with laurel, ivy, opium, tobacco, or innumerable other vegetable substances gained from fruits, leaves, tubers and seeds" sets in motion "a natural potency of the female psyche, through which from time immemorial woman, in her character of sibyl, priestess and wise woman, has influenced mankind." He goes on to say, "And over and over again we find this mantic woman connected with the symbols of cauldron and cave, of night and moon." All this may be true, but it is well to keep in mind that divination is about equally divided between male and female practitioners and that the cauldron belongs to Odin as well as to Caridwen and the Weirds.

To Robert Graves, Caridwen's stew pot is the "Cauldron of Inspiration," and here I agree with him. The gist of the story is simple enough, and its relation to shamanistic usage seems obvious. According to the tale, the Welsh witch Caridwen put a cauldron full of knowledge on to boil; then, leaving a blind man to feed the fire and the boy Gwion to stir the pot, she went out on the hills to gather more herbs for her brew. As Gwion stirred, three drops of liquor splashing out of the pot burned his finger. When he put his finger in his mouth to ease the pain, he tasted the brew and thereupon became possessed of all knowledge. Henceforth he is not Gwion, but Taliesin, a poet. He has learned among other things the art of shape-shifting; in his flight from the enraged

Caridwen, both he and she change into animals at will.

The Celtic pot corresponds to the Norse cauldron called Odrörir. Odin acquired shamanistic powers when he drank from it, because it contained the blood of Kvasir to whom the gods had given all knowledge. Inspired poets, whose wisdom is close to occult knowledge, are indebted to Odin for the mead he gives them from the cauldron. Bad poets get only the drops that Odin spilled when he stole the mead from Suttungr. Odin, like Taliesin, is a shape-shifter; it is one of the characteristics that identifies him as a shaman god.

The cauldron, then, belongs to the mantic male as well as the female, and I think we may take it that the contents of the cauldron are related to the actual potion sipped by the seer as the shaman god is related to the shaman. Odrörir, who is a person as well as a vessel, might be compared to the Tamyush of the Luiseno Indians, which (or who) is a stone bowl in which the ceremonial jimsonweed drink is mixed; at the same time it is one of the Earth People, born of the Earth Mother.

Since all prophecy is concerned with the future, time concepts are important to the prophetic tradition; certain times are considered suitable to the forecasting of events. The two times most often mentioned for the appearance of the Fates are the time of birth and the beginning of a year. The fairy godmothers and the Seven Hathors appear at the birth of a child to foretell its destiny. The deities presiding at the birth seem to be always feminine, naturally enough, while the god who fixed the fates at the New Year in the ancient Near East was a male.

Charles Leland, whose book of Algonquin legends was published in 1884, said flatly that shamanism was the world's first religion. The more we learn, the less we

think we know; perhaps no one would be brash enough
to make such a statement today. I should not care to do
so, but I confess I often wonder whether Leland was
right. Soothsaying is of course only one aspect of shamanism. In certain societies specialization has gone so
far that the roles of diviner, medium, herbalist and
exorcist are divided among as many different experts.
In the beginning, we have reason to think that they
were one, and that the shaman played all the roles, as
he (or she) does in some cultures today.

Despite my reservations with regard to the passage
quoted above from Erich Neumann, I would agree that
women have practiced shamanism as much as men, and
perhaps even earlier. If it is true, as we are often told,
that they were the gatherers of fruit and herbs when
men turned to hunting, perhaps their acquaintance with
narcotic plants led them directly into the professions of
healing and soothsaying. The Norns, the Fates, and possibly even the Sibyls are older and more powerful than
the gods themselves. The sisters around their cauldron
raise more questions of the past than they ever answered
about the future.

9) Grandfather Pleiades
and other ancestors

Mythologists have tried repeatedly since ancient times to answer a still vexing question: Where do the gods come from? We have had a variety of answers, most of them probably right for some god, somewhere. No one answer will account for all the deities in a single polytheistic society, perhaps not even for all the aspects of a single deity. In other chapters I have called attention to gods whose origin is relatively clear, for example certain deified intoxicants and drug plants. There are also deities of time and space, earth and sky; there are shaman gods: deities of healing, death and destiny. The deified hero and the deified ancestor, once popular candidates for the role of protogod, have rather fallen out of favor, partly because their adherents tried to hold the historical line, an impossible position.

William Ridgeway, in two books, *The Origin of Tragedy* and *Dramas and Dramatic Dances* (1915), made one of the last really formidable attempts to trace *all* the gods to actual men and women who had undergone apotheosis after death. Although the work is now known chiefly through subsequent attacks on it, like the scathing references in Lord Raglan's *The Hero,* the two schools of thought represented by Ridgeway and Lord Raglan do have one thing in common. Ridgeway puts his emphasis on the apotheosis of the historical hero through burial rites and ceremonies in honor of the dead. To Lord Raglan, on the other hand, a myth is a narrative describing remembered ritual. In both arguments rite is the catalyst: in one it changes historical events into myths; in the other the enactment of a rite produces a myth where none was before. What *was* there before is the question.

When a mythologist uses the word "rite" he usually means an act intended to produce magical or supernatural results. It may be anything from circumambulation to human sacrifice. However, the newspaper tells us of "rites" held at the opening of new bridges, launching of new ships, dedication of new post offices, and so on. A "rite" seems to be any occasion that calls for band music, flowers, flags, dedicatory speeches, or the wearing of special headgear. "Ceremony" would be a better word if it were not too long for the headlines. Ceremonies may be either sacred or secular, whereas the word "rite" implies at least the presence of a clergyman. Some mythologists might argue that the ribbon-cutting ceremony is only a last, desanctified vestige of superstitious rites in which sacrificed children were buried in the foundations of bridges. All ceremony, according to their reasoning, is in its origin religious, secular ceremonies being survivals of ancient ritual which in turn had its primitive—or instinctive—beginning in sympathetic magic.

Today in our society it is true that ceremonies are unnecessary. Students can graduate from college without parading in cap and gown; the *act,* or rite, matters much less than the information on a punchcard in the Dean's office. It is also true that in any society where the political and social structure is inseparable from the religious structure, every ceremony is religious. However, just for the mental exercise if nothing else, will the reader please try to imagine a preliterate community with a rudimentary social structure and *no* religion, and ask himself whether it would function without ceremony?

Its "rites" might be simply ceremonies of definition corresponding to graduation exercises, with one difference: in the absence of written documents the overt act in the presence of witnesses is a necessity rather than a gratuitous flourish of trumpets. The printed, punched, signed and sealed documents, certificates, and licenses of our society take the place of ancient ceremonies in which the boy became a man, the man became the head of a family, the warrior became a chieftain or a member of the tribal council. Ceremonies defined the relationships between members of families and members of the society as a whole. They signified the privileges and responsibilities of the position the individual occupied in the community. The regalia that goes with office is another form of definition. It may be only a leopard skin or bunch of feathers on the end of a pole; it may have no more religious significance than the college freshman's green cap, but like the green cap it is a custom. Who started the custom of the bunch of feathers on a pole? The members of my hypothetical preliterate society, having no religion, and having inherited the tradition of the feathered pole, assume (probably correctly) that their ancestors originated the customs and insignia that serve not only to distinguish one member of the group from another, but also to set the group itself apart from the neighboring tribes or communities. The inherited tradition is convenient but not absolutely sacrosanct. Traditions and customs do change gradually in all societies, but they also tend to gather unto themselves superstitions and even to assume a sacred character. If we were to encounter my hypothetical society at this stage of its development, I wonder whether we should recognize it as a community devoid of religion? Or has it acquired a religion without knowing what has happened?

Perhaps the answer hinges on whether or not the people in question recognize a deity. They have customs to which they cling, for reasons indicated above; they have inherited traditions; if they have a ruler, the ruler must operate within the tradition. Somebody supervises the ceremonies to see that they do not deviate from tradition. Behind all the activities performed in accordance with unwritten laws is an abstract power respected by the members of the society; personified it is the tribal deity or law god, perhaps with the face and name of the ultimate ancestor.

The importance of the ancestor god lies not at all in his historical actuality, but in his role as author; he is author of customs, laws, traditions, and even of life itself. The ancestor may be worshiped, or he may simply figure in mythology; he may be conceived as active in the affairs of the tribe; he may be impersonated, for example in the dance dramas described by Ridgeway. In any case we should quite certainly say of his people that they had a religion, although we might qualify it as a state religion or limit it to "ancestor worship." I do not know whether any deity ever did take shape in this way. I only say he could have.

Ridgeway, however, put great emphasis on burial rites, and in this I suppose him to be correct. Some of the earliest ceremonies ever devised by men were presumably those connected with disposal of the dead. Again, we have to give due credit to necessity as the mother, or perhaps the grandmother of ceremony. Dead bodies must be disposed of somehow, and a customary method of disposition has probably developed in every community regardless of religious beliefs. For each society there is one right way to do a thing compared with a number of wrong ways. The right way can easily become elaborated bit by bit until it is a traditional ceremony, even without belief in life after death. The graves of prehistoric men tell us very little about belief although in many cases they suggest ceremonial disposal of the dead.

However, a belief in the continued existence of the disembodied soul is known to be widespread and probably very early indeed. Many societies have annual rites when all the dead are honored—that is, all the ancestors. Sometimes the dead are said to be present on these occasions; sometimes they are impersonated by descendants or masqueraders; sometimes a shaman communicates with the dead by going into a trance. We can find parallels for all these acts in funeral customs also; and in either case, they contribute to the mythology of the ancestor and the afterlife.

The myths of the ancestor god are as diverse as the

societies that acknowledge his existence. Ancestor myths are especially important in shaman societies, where the office of shaman is often hereditary, and the techniques of shamanism are said to have been taught originally by the ancestor god with whom the shaman is still in communication. Where the shaman in trance makes animal sounds and movements, the ancestor spirit easily assumes animal form. There are even stellar ancestor gods, and that among a people as destitute of material culture as the Abipones of Paraguay. Frazer cited this example, but only in an appendix, and Ridgeway missed or ignored it—after all, a Pleiades ancestor does little to establish the historical reality of ancestor gods in general.

The Pleiades ancestor, who had no apparent connection with fertility magic, baffled Frazer as much as he baffled the missionary, Father Dobrizhoffer, from whom Frazer took his account. The brief description in *The Golden Bough* (vii, 308) tells of a drinkfest held each year at the first rising of the Pleiades after their period of invisibility (in May). When the constellation was sighted, the Abipones happily saluted it with flutes and drums, and congratulated their ancestor on his recovery from "illness." In celebration of his return, they collected wild honey, brewed a favorite drink, and spent the whole night in revelry presided over by a sorceress who shook a rattle and danced. Frazer, losing interest, concludes: "But the proceedings were perfectly decorous; the sexes did not mix with each other."

The relevant facts given by Father Dobrizhoffer in some detail are these:

The Abipones had no religion except shamanism, and no deity other than Grandfather Pleiades, who had taught them shamanism. The drinkfest described was the occasion for annual ceremonies when new shamans, both male and female, were initiated. The heliacal rising of the Pleiades gave the signal for the festival, and the constellation was accordingly identified with the ancestor to whose teaching they attributed their only rites. The identification with the Pleiades was as reasonable as an identification of the ancestor with the moon, or even the sun. It is not without parallel in other parts of South America, and in Polynesia as well, where the Pukapukans called themselves "descendants of the Pleiades." They, too, used the heliacal rising of that constellation as their signal for annual shaman ceremonies and the beginning of the New Year.

Two elements—the calendar and the ceremonies associated with the dead (in this case through shamanism)—have combined to form the stellar ancestor god. Other elements combine to form other gods; but everywhere ceremony of some sort is acting as a catalyst, precipitating both gods and myths. One of the greatest errors we can make, as I see it, is to assume that only one kind of ceremony is at work; and the most prevalent minor error is the assumption that every ceremony is originally performed out of an instinctive belief in its supernatural efficacy.

PART IV

10)   Second thoughts on egg symbolism

To the hen an egg is not a symbol; we must assume that
to her an egg is an egg. To our remote ancestors, before
symbolism was thought of, an egg must have been,
again, an egg, a thing peculiarly itself. To the modern
student of symbolism, however, the egg is an object of
profound significance. It is the Cosmic Egg, or the Egg
of Creation floating on a primeval sea. It is the egg
symbol of Fertility, the Easter egg, or a Moon egg. In
mythology it is the Swan's egg found (or produced) by
Leda, the egg from which the Twins were hatched. It is
the Swallow's egg that dropped into the mouth of
Chien-Ti and caused her pregnancy. It is the World Egg
of the *Upanishads*, or the Orphic egg from which Phanes

emerged at the beginning of Time. Occasionally we need to pause and remind ourselves that the symbolism does not itself produce the egg; the egg was there before any symbolism became attached to it.

The most popular assumption about egg symbolism is that the egg, being a stage in the reproductive process, is a fertility symbol. In other words, the collective wish, conscious or unconscious, for fertility in all its forms (crops, cattle, offspring, sexual activity) clothes itself in the image of the egg, which is thereupon introduced into the ritual play of the society. Egg symbolism, however, has other elements often overlooked. Both the bird and the egg have explicit associations with time and the calendar, and so with the timing of festivals. Eliade has pointed to the egg as symbolic of the renewal associated with the New Year, which is perfectly true if the New Year falls at egg time, otherwise not.

Much has been written in the last two or three decades concerning the psychological importance of the New Year and the re-creation through New Year ritual of the world as it was at the beginning of time. Now I agree that the New Year is likely to be the most important annual festival in a primitive calendar. It is, besides, necessarily the *first* of the annual festivals, a fact less often stressed but one to keep in mind. Although any one of the 365 days of the year may serve as a date for an annual feast day, some method must be devised to distinguish that day from its fellows; and whenever one day is set aside to mark the completion of the annual round, that day is New Year's Day. It may also be a feast of the dead, or a day for initiating new shamans; it may be a day for rewards and punishments; for gift giving, making visits, collecting taxes, or getting drunk.

The traditions that accumulate around the celebration of the New Year are secondary to the perception of the round of the seasons, and they follow upon the fixing of a date to mark the completion of one round and the beginning of the other.

The fixing of a date is itself dependent upon a signal, celestial, animal, or vegetable, or perhaps upon a combination of signals. New Year's Day may fall in any season. It may even rotate through the tropical year, but this is a complication we need not go into here. The curious reader can find discussions of nontropical years elsewhere, but the egg signal that has fixed a New Year's date in at least two simple calendars is a fascinating and little-known piece of calendar history. Furthermore, it sheds some needed light on the question—too often treated simply rhapsodically—of egg symbolism.

The two calendars are the tern-egg calendar of the Easter Islanders and the palolo-egg calendar of Fiji. The tern is of course a sea bird; the palolo, almost unknown except for its peculiar spawning habits, is a sea worm.

When Easter Island was first discovered by Europeans, three barren islets just off the coast of the main island served as rookeries for the sooty tern. The search for the first tern's egg laid each spring on the islet of Motu-nui was the major event of Easter Island's liturgical year, as well as the most elaborate egg hunt ever staged by any people. The preliminary ceremonies began in July when the chieftains who were to participate went in procession to the village of Orongo on a headland overlooking Motu-nui; in August their servants, braving sharks and rocky surf, swam out to the islet, where they waited and watched, often for weeks, for a tern to lay an egg. Meanwhile elaborate ceremonies were conducted at Orongo where the chieftains kept vigil. When at last a bird obliged by laying an egg, the fortunate finder bound the egg to his forehead and swam back to the main island. This first egg was symbolic of the New Year and the good fortune the New Year is supposed to bring. The egg was the embodiment, for one year's time, of the god Make-make, the Creator-god of Easter Island, a deity corresponding to Tane or Kane of the other Polynesians. The chieftain whose servant found the first-laid egg became the Bird-man of that year and *gave his name to the year*. He himself, as well as the egg, was a year symbol. The egg was blown, filled with tapa, and suspended in the hut where the Bird-man lived alone, surrounded by tabus, until the year's end; then the egg, having lost its power, was thrown into the sea and replaced by the new Year-egg. At the end of his term the Bird-man resumed a normal existence and, when he died, was buried in a special cemetery reserved for Bird-men. The half-subterranean stone houses of Orongo where the prolonged ceremonies were held are still decorated with petroglyphs of Bird-men and eggs, as are the cave shelters of Motu-nui. The name the Bird-man gave the year was a ceremonial name that was revealed to him in a dream at the time of his success; the bird cult was, as Métraux says, in effect the basis for a convenient chronological system. Perhaps I should add that the name of the island is only a happy coincidence. Easter Island was first sighted on Easter Sunday, 1722, that is approximately at the time of the first full moon following the vernal equinox in the northern hemisphere. The Easter Island egg hunt had its culmination in September, near the time of the vernal equinox in the southern hemisphere. Egg symbolism in general has an affinity for festivals falling at the spring equinox, whether the spring season comes in September or March.

Before I say more about bird eggs, let me go on to the fish eggs. The palolo (also spelled bololo, mbololo and mbalolo) lives in the coral reefs of the South Seas. The major spawning period or Big Palolo lasts only a few hours; it begins at dawn at neap tide at the third quarter of the October-November moon. At the moment when the swarming is expected the Fiji Islanders are out in the lagoons in their canoes waiting for the first appearance of the palolo, or so at least it was when Alexander Agassiz wrote his eyewitness account of a palolo New Year from which I have taken my notes. At one moment, he says, the water was perfectly clear; a few moments later the first palolo appeared and the Islanders began to dip them out; very soon the water in the lagoons was as "thick as vermicelli soup" with spawning sea worms which had to be seized before they discharged their roe. Suddenly the spawning was over, and the Islanders went home with their catch. That day they feasted on palolo eggs served warm and wrapped in banana leaves, a New Year's Day dinner.

These two examples of the egg-triggered calendar have interesting points in common, and possibly even more interesting points of contrast. A prolonged period of watching and waiting was unnecessary in Fiji because the palolo swarming was timed exactly by moon and tide. True, the date of the swarming moved about, by our calendar, just as Easter moves; it fell a little earlier each year for two years in succession, then skipped back into November as the palolo's timing mechanism intercalated the thirteenth moon, harmonizing the lunar and solar cycles. The Fiji Islanders, being well acquainted with lunar and tidal phenomena, knew when to look for

the spawning worms. If they did not appear at the third
quarter of the twelfth moon, they could be depended
upon to appear next month at the same time. They also
used other phenomena—a blossoming tree, for instance
—as a signal that the Big Palolo was approaching. Constellations and star names were likewise associated with
the palolo catch; the position of certain stars gave warning of the Palolo Moon.

Neither the bird nor the sea worm had the slightest
economic importance; as a source of food supply the
value of each was negligible if not nonexistent. The
value of the tern's egg was a superstitious one acquired
through its use as a year symbol, yet the petroglyphs
are monuments to the large role it played in the culture
of Easter Island. The palolo has not influenced Melanesian iconography so far as I know; neither the worm nor
the roe lends itself to representational art. For that matter, although the palolo is widely known in Melanesia,
and has left its mark on more than one Melanesian calendar, I cannot point with confidence to any corresponding use of spawning fish. Except for an occasional sea
serpent's egg, the mythology and folklore of the egg is
concerned usually with fowl's eggs.

The Moslem calendar, unlike the palolo calendar, takes
no notice of the intercalary thirteenth moon, but oper-
ates on a straight twelve-moon schedule, with a New
Year that rotates through the seasons. *That* New Year
could never have carried with it the ancient usage of the
egg hunt. However, in defiance of Mohammed's calendar, the pre-Moslem Nawruz of the Zoroastrians, a festival falling at the spring equinox, has survived the
intervening centuries and even spread into other Moslem countries. If, as Eliade says, it is also called the

Feast of Red Eggs, the name would tell us the season of the festival had we no other clue. The Easter egg is associated with Easter rather than Halloween, Christmas, or New Year's, because Easter comes at egg-laying time, near the spring equinox.

Of all the birds credited with the annunciation of spring, the cuckoo, the dove, and the swallow seem to have had the widest vogue. The one swallow that does not make a summer is nevertheless the herald of summer's approach. Swallows return, not all at once, to be sure, but rather punctually to their nesting places in many parts of the world. San Juan Capistrano has no monopoly of swallow folklore. Ancient China celebrated each spring a royal festival known as the "Day of the Swallow's Return." On this day, according to an old legend, one of the returning swallows dropped an egg into the mouth of a lady named Chien-Ti. She became pregnant by the swallow's egg and gave birth (presumably at the winter solstice) to the Dark King, founder of the Shang dynasty. Another version of the story says that she won the egg in a tournament. Arthur Waley calls the story of Chien-Ti "a typical Eastern Chinese origin myth. The ruling family of Ch'in, which came from eastern China, gave an almost identical account of their origin." Tradition does not say that the festival was a New Year festival, but only that it was held at the spring equinox.

The dynastic-origin stories (in which category I should include that of Leda and the swan's egg from which the sons of Zeus were hatched) lead directly into the creation stories. The Maoris tell of a bird that dropped an egg into the primeval sea. When the egg broke, a man, a woman, a boy, a girl, a pig, a dog, and a canoe came out of the egg; the people and animals got into the canoe and drifted to New Zealand. The Cahuilla Indians of California said that the world was created by two brothers who hatched from two large eggs that appeared in the void. The Finnish egg-of-creation, as described in the *Kalevala,* is a teal's egg, laid with six others in a nest on the upraised knee of a floating goddess. When the nest fell and the egg broke, the sun was formed of its yolk, the moon from the egg white, the stars from the speckled parts, and so on. This egg has a parallel in the cosmic egg of the *Mahabharata,* an egg which was itself "the first cause, a mighty egg, the one inexhaustible seed of all created beings. From this egg proceeded [the gods], the waters, the heavens, the earth, the sky, the points of heaven, the years and seasons, with day and night in due succession. Thus were produced all things known to man." In the Hindu writings the egg has created itself; no bird dropped it on the sea or laid it in a floating nest. The chicken-and-egg problem that remains unsolved is the relative priority of the cosmic archetypal Egg from which all creation proceeded, and the egg that serves as year symbol: the real and tangible egg, laid by a real bird, hunted at the spring equinox. This is a problem that is unlikely to be solved to the satisfaction of all students of symbolism. The Polynesian tradition illustrates the difficulties: besides the Maori story mentioned above, there are other stories of the egg-of-creation. From the Society Islands there comes the statement that, "In the beginning, Taaroa existed in an egg, in darkness, from which he later burst forth." From Hawaii we hear that "a bird laid an egg upon the primeval waters and this afterwards burst of itself and produced the world." On the basis of the similarity between these traditions and that found in the Sanskrit

writings, some scholars have surmised that the Polynesian myth was influenced by the Hindu cosmology, by
way of Indonesia. The Easter Islanders are, of course,
Polynesians who might be supposed to have carried the
myth to their remote outpost, and developed the ritual
egg hunt as an accompaniment to the myth. As it happens, however, the myth has not been reported from
Easter Island, and no other Polynesians have egg-hunt
ceremonies corresponding to those of Easter Island's
bird cult.

So far as the Polynesians are concerned, the myth-
and-egg problem will probably remain unsolved. However, even if we could with any certainty trace the egg
hunt back to the Hindu creation myth, we should still
have to postulate a previous acquaintance with eggs on
the part of the mythmaker. The real egg comes first in any
case; I should surmise that the equinoctial festival comes
next, and the myth of the cosmic egg-of-creation last.

In the first canto of the *Inferno,* Dante says that the
stars now rising with the sun (on Good Friday in the
year 1300, the date of his journey through the universe)
are the same that rose with the sun at the creation. In
other words, the world was created, according to the
tradition he followed, at the spring equinox. Nothing in
the universe demands that the creation should have
taken place at that season, but here the association of
the creation myth with the New Year ritual becomes
pertinent. Many calendar makers have shown a preference for a New Year falling at or near the spring equinox.
The creation of the world, the beginning of time, and
the first day of the calendar year not unnaturally coin-
cide. If the festival is timed by new or full moon, a
coalescence of symbolism may give rise to legends of
the bird-egg, the full-moon-egg, and the egg-of-creation.

The swan's egg or swallow's egg of mythology is the egg of the equinoctial festival. The New Year egg may contain the luck of the year, like that of Easter Island: good crops, good fishing, good weather, good fortune, or, as Frazer would have said, Fertility.

11) Eclipse

Myths of eclipses, either of the sun or moon, are usually
classed as etiological myths—that is, they are stories explaining a natural phenomenon. The sun is in eclipse
because it is being swallowed by a dragon: that sort of
thing. As a class these myths merge with fables telling
why the crow is black or how the leopard got his spots.
Many eclipse myths, however, are etiological in another
sense: they explain why people do certain things on
certain occasions. They are still "why" stories, but the
fact that they explain an action performed by members
of a human society takes them out of the animal fable
class altogether and relates them rather to what is sometimes called a "true" myth. A true myth is difficult to

define; we usually mean a myth important enough to warrant serious study. Its importance lies partly in its apparent influence on human behavior and partly in the wide distribution of the theme.

Certain tales from India might serve as exemplars of the second type of eclipse myth, for instance a story reported from Bombay where alms are traditionally given to the Mang caste at the time of eclipse. The sun, in this case, is said to be endangered by the importunities of an untouchable Mang woman. The shadow is cast by a basket in which she carries the head of her son, who was killed by Rama during a victory feast. The alms given to the Mang caste are intended to appease the Mang woman in the sky. In the Central Provinces, where alms were given to street sweepers at the time of eclipse, it was said that the sun owes a sweeper (Rahu, the eclipse demon) a debt he refuses to pay. The sweeper sits at the sun's door and casts his shadow on the sun. The alms are intended to appease the sweeper-god, Rahu.

Here, in these two simple stories, we have one of the crucial problems faced by every mythologist. Does the myth in fact influence behavior or does the behavior give rise to the myth? An expert on India and Hindu mythology might be able to answer positively. My tentative answer is that, in these cases at least, the behavior gives rise to the myth. Rahu, the eclipse demon, has been familiar to Hindus for more than two millennia. So far as I am aware, he is a street sweeper, or a sweeper-god, only in those regions where alms are given to sweepers at the time of the eclipse. The story of the Mang woman is peculiar to the region where alms are given to the Mang caste at that time. The alms-giving is the common denominator, and is only one of several acts associated with the eclipse. The eclipse may be said to determine the time for the alms-giving, as Christmas has been a traditional time for alms-giving in the West.

The giving of alms at eclipse time is a rarity. So are ceremonial bathing and the offering of all one's possessions to the moon. Fasting, feasting, praying, or the singing of songs are more usual activities, but the most widespread of all is noisemaking. About half the eclipse myths I have been able to collect were told in explanation of the noise that people are obliged or permitted to make at that time. Most of the explanations involve an attack on the sun or moon, depending on which is being darkened. The only thing they have in common with the Hindu stories just referred to is the idea that the sun is threatened.

There is a story from Annam to the effect that eclipses of the moon are caused by an enormous moon-eating toad which the Lord of the Han Lake keeps chained on the lake bottom. Occasionally, when the god is sleeping, the toad breaks his chain and escapes. He straightway makes for the moon and swallows it. The Moon Girls, who guide the moon across the sky, then run to waken the toad's keeper; and it is to help them that young women everywhere make a racket by striking pestles on rice mortars. The Lord of the Han Lake, being roused by the clatter, rescues the moon and rechains the toad on the lake bottom.

The notion that the noise is designed to awaken someone who will rescue the moon is also rather unusual. The more familiar explanation is that the row made by beating on pots and pans, gongs and drums, will drive off the animal or evil spirit that is swallowing the sun or moon. In a story told by the Todas a snake is pursuing not the moon itself but a hare. This hare, fleeing for its life, went to the sun, but the sun warned him off because of the heat, and told him to go to the moon. When the hare went to the moon, the moon said, "Do not be afraid; I will protect you till the end of the world." The snake still goes sometimes to catch the hare in the moon, and when he does the moon becomes dark; some people fire guns and send up rockets; the Todas shout. They also abstain from food on days of both solar and lunar eclipses; after the solar eclipse they have a feast.

The study of eclipse myths can quickly degenerate into a study of superstitions: people do thus and so because they believe a snake is swallowing the moon. Perhaps, indeed, they do. When we ask why they believe anything so unlikely, we are told that it is perfectly natural; "primitive," untutored, preliterate or illiterate people everywhere do believe that a snake or dog is swallowing the moon whenever an eclipse occurs. After all, an eclipse to them is an inexplicable and terrifying event. They are scared out of their very simple wits, and they *see* the dog or dragon swallowing the sun or moon.

In the happy days before I began to think about mythology I could swallow this story as easily as the moon toad swallows the moon. What would the ignorant savage think of the sun's eclipse except that the world was coming to an end? The answer is, of course, that he would think the sun was in eclipse. Eclipses are not once-in-a-lifetime occurrences. The child who first experiences the darkening of the sun has a parent to tell him that this is an eclipse—quick! grab a pan and beat on it! There would be no tradition of a moon toad or noisemaking at eclipse time if the knowledge of eclipses were not also traditional. Furthermore, eclipses of the moon are at least as important to mythology as eclipses of the sun, yet the occasional passage of a murky, red-

dish shadow across the face of the full moon should not
be especially terrifying, and actually seems to be an
occasion for celebration rather than panic. In a description of an eclipse of the moon as observed in Brazil
among the naked Urubus, Francis Huxley says: "Besides
carnival, there was another excuse for making a lot of
noise at the post: there was an eclipse of the moon."
For two hours everyone "honored the occasion with traditional salutes: ringing bells, blowing whistles and
horns, drumming on the iron roof of the manioc house,
pounding the floor boards and letting off musket shots."
The Urubus seemed to Huxley to be enjoying the occasion, much as Americans enjoy making a racket on the
stroke of midnight, December 31st, and probably for
the same reasons whatever they are. A description
of Chinese coolies celebrating an eclipse of the moon
around the turn of the century is exactly parallel to this:
the same racket, the same enjoyment of the racket.

I shall return later to the fear especially associated
with eclipses of the sun, but first there is an important
point to be made about eclipses in general. A man who
reads time in the sky *may* be better informed about
eclipses than the literate city dweller whose calendar
hangs on the wall. In preliterate societies the days are
almost always counted by the phases of the moon. The
most important dates in the calendar are usually, therefore, full moon, new moon, and dark of the moon.
Eclipses of the moon occur only at full moon and eclipses
of the sun fall, naturally, only at dark of the moon, when
the moon passes across the face of the sun in the day-
time. Since the calendar maker is a moon-watcher, he
can hardly fail to notice that eclipses always come at
full moon and dark of the moon. He knows approximately where the moon is at the time of an eclipse of

the sun, and he is likely to know as well as you or I that the time of eclipse is a time when the sun and moon meet.

Some myths of the sun's eclipse are metaphors that describe the meeting. The same people who told the story of the moon toad also said that the Moon Girls who guided the moon along the moon's path and the Sun Boys who did the same for the sun sometimes met at a crossing of the paths; here the girls spread their veils to conceal the rendezvous from peeping eyes and thus caused the eclipse of the sun. More often myths of this sort, describing the meeting of sun and moon, make the two husband and wife, or brother and sister, the sister fleeing from the incestuous love of her brother, and so on. Some Polynesians say the stars are the children of sun and moon, born of the intercourse that takes place during the sun's eclipse. The same sort of story is of course never told of an eclipse of the moon because at that time the moon and sun are at the opposite ends of the sky; it is the earth's shadow that moves across the face of the full moon and causes the eclipse of her light, although the moon itself remains visible.

Shakespeare speaks of the moon as "sick almost to doomsday with eclipse," a figure of speech more apt than the swallowing image as a description of the moon at eclipse time. The same observation has been made by the Indians of Peru, who used to say that the moon was sick during her eclipse, and, when she recovered her light, that she had been healed by Pachamac. The Chiquitos, also of South America, say she has been hunted by dogs, but instead of being swallowed by them, she has been torn "until her light is reddened and quenched by blood." These Indians raise a din and shoot arrows into the sky (also an ancient Chinese custom) to drive off the dogs. But North American Indians launched fire-tipped arrows at the sky to relight the sun after its eclipse.

In the examples given above I have tried to show that, while eclipse myths are a far cry from astronomical science, they may be metaphors based on direct observation of eclipses. They vary. The eclipse demon is widespread, but not inevitable, and it takes many forms. The Polynesians in Mangaia used to say that there were two; one came from the east to swallow the moon, one from the west to swallow the sun. This, again, is an example of correct observation, since the moon moves across the face of the sun from west to east, and the earth's shadow passes over the moon's face from east to west. Some say the eclipse demon is a star; the Bagobos (in the Philippines) say it is a huge bird that swallows the moon during eclipse, and will swallow the sun and all the people on the earth as well unless it can be persuaded to open its mouth and disgorge the moon "—a result which is regularly brought about by the shouting and screaming of men, and the beating of agongs."

One of my favorite eclipse monsters is the Hindu Rahu, already mentioned. Rahu is a character in the famous myth that tells how the gods and demons together used a mountain as a churn stick, churning furiously until they were able to produce the *amṛta,* or ambrosia, a drink of immortality. When the churning was at last successful and the bowl of elixir was produced, the gods appropriated it. During the feast that followed, the demon Rahu attempted to steal the precious beverage. He took a great gulp, but the liquid had got only as far as his throat when the god Indra hurled his discus and took off Rahu's head. Since then the head has carried on alone as the moon's ascending node

(*caput draconis*) which is in everlasting pursuit of the
moon and sun, and sometimes swallows one or the other.
This famous literary myth from the *Mahabharata* may
be compared with a Burmese folktale telling how the
moon stole a pestle that had the secret of immortality.
A dog pursues the moon and tries to steal the pestle.
Occasionally the dog manages to catch the moon, but
when he does he finds it too large to swallow, and lets it
go again. The moon is made immortal by the power of
the pestle, and the dog itself is kept alive by the pestle's
odor. When we know that the Hindu's sacred draught of
soma was prepared with mortar and pestle, that it was
considered to be a food of immortality for both gods and
men, and that it was identified with the moon, the latter
story seems a homely variant of the more elaborate
theme from the literary epic.

The truth is that the diffusion of the eclipse monster
from one part of the world to another is an awkward
possibility rarely mentioned. No one would be surprised
to find variants of the Rahu story in Burma or in Indian
folktales (for instance, that head in the basket). The hare
in the moon mentioned in the Toda story is well known
throughout the Orient. In China the hare is pounding
the elixir of immortality with mortar and pestle. The
toad in the moon is depicted in Chinese art of the Han
period and later: it is the goddess Heng O, who stole
the elixir of immortality, floated up to the moon and was
changed into a toad. But whether this toad is any sort
of cousin to the moon toad of Annam, or whether the
pestle in the Burmese story is related to that of the
Chinese moon hare, we do not know. We cannot know
whether the eclipse demons and the din they occasion
have traveled from, say, China to Kamchatka to the
New World. What we do know is that eclipses were

being studied in China as early as the time of the Shang dynasty (about the fourteenth century B.C. and following). The records found on the oracle bones indicate that they were being studied for reasons having to do with time and the exact period of the lunations rather than for astrological reasons. Astrological reasons in themselves have to do with time, though in a superstitious sense. And this brings me to my final point about eclipse myths and the fear of eclipse.

Shakespeare remarks that the moon is sick almost to "doomsday"; the hare in the moon will be protected "until the end of the world"; if the Bagobo bird were not frightened off, it would swallow the whole world as well as the sun and moon. Eclipses are linked with cataclysms in South America, where it is said that an "Eternal Bat" will devour the sun and moon at the end of the world. The Norse Eddas tell how the sun and moon will be swallowed by the Fenris wolf at the Doom of the Gods, and so on. Not long ago thousands of people, according to the news reports, were braced for the world's end during an eclipse of the sun when all the planets met in one Zodiacal sign. These are myths or old wives' tales or superstitions, but all are directly related to time-telling. The explanation is this: time is, but time must have had a start, and is frequently thought to have a stop. The starting, and therefore the stopping also, takes place when the time-telling luminaries are precisely joined, when the two hands of the clock stand one upon the other and point to twelve midnight. Eclipse time is midnight, and the noisemaking is best understood, as I have already pointed out, by relating it to our New Year racket. The apprehension is akin to the apprehension felt by the Aztecs when the Pleiades passed over the meridian at midnight at the end of the Aztec 52-year cycle. They did not really expect the world to end at that moment, I imagine, but they had the happy assurance that if it did not end then, it would be safe for another fifty-two years.

Now to come back to my original proposition: eclipse myths are not only etiological myths explaining a natural phenomenon, but they are myths explaining what people do, and as such they have an importance for the study of mythology. The activities are varied: arrow-shooting, noisemaking, fasting, feasting, singing, alms-giving. The explanations for these activities are also various, and while I have not done an exhaustive study and tabulated the results, my impression is that the explanations vary more than the activities. The activities are sometimes associated with other occasions such as new or full moon, or the New Year. We may ask, then, whether people make noises and shoot arrows because they believe thus and so, or whether they invent the myths to accompany, program, costume, or explain their actions? Are the fire-tipped arrows in the nature of primitive fireworks or are they really believed to be essential to the relighting of the sun? It is easier for me to accept the existence of a spontaneous impulse to mark by some action the time of the eclipse, than it is to credit a spontaneous belief in eclipse demons. In this respect I suppose I am something of an oddity. I should say, however, that no doubt the observation and activity together give rise to the belief, that the belief in turn colors the activity, and that all three mingling produce the mythology of eclipses.

12) The dancing stars

A few years ago I used to drop in occasionally on the afternoon lecture at a famous planetarium. As a part of the program the lecturer pointed out to us, while we craned our necks in the darkness, the constellations moving across the domed ceiling. When he came to the Pleiades, he would say: "And here are the Pleiades, usually called the *seven* Pleiades; nobody knows why, unless because there are only six." The joke always raised a laugh, and what were the children there for if not to be entertained? He did not tell his audience that the "missing" seventh Pleiad is visible today through a telescope and may once have been as bright as the others. In my experience his attitude is typical of most contemporary astronomers, to whom a star myth is a capricious invention of no possible interest unless it can be made to emphasize the long way we have come since the days when stars were believed to be people, or gods, or ghosts of the dead. I can sympathize with the astronomer's lack of interest; he has other fish to fry. The comparative mythologists, however, tend to be equally neglectful, perhaps in part because they are ignorant of or indifferent to the raw first principles of time-keeping. Also, reputable scholars are frightened off the subject by their distrust of astrologers, Pan-Babylonians, Rosicrucians and lay writers of mystical bent who have given star myths a bad name. In this brief exploration of Pleiades mythology I shall try to avoid the worst traps. Granted that the stargazer's foot often slips, still there is a certain security in the calendar and its uses. These last are neither mystical nor (to any great extent) debatable; they take some of the silliness out of star myths and may even shed light on mythology in general.

The first question that star myths raise in my mind is this: by what process does a faraway twinkling point of light become a mythical personality? About 9000 stars are visible to the naked eye, and some 2000 of these can be seen at one time from one part of the earth. Of the thousands of visible stars only a few have figured in mythology. Fewer still have been personified or worshiped. A casual glance at the heavens will never tell us why those few have been chosen, or which have taken first rank among them. Only a correlation of the mythology with customs, calendars and astronomical data can suggest plausible answers.

For a beginning, let us look at a simple statement in which personality is at least implied. The Maoris of New

Zealand reported to early inquirers a rivalry between the Pleiades and Rigel (β Orionis). Rigel, they said, was hostile to the Pleiades because he wished to rule the year himself. In the northern part of New Zealand, Rigel did in fact rule the year, since the heliacal (morning) rising of that star was the signal for a New Year celebration. In the south, as generally throughout Polynesia, the Pleiades, called Matariki, performed the same function. The occasion of the rising of the Pleiades, we are told, "was marked by a festival, by feasting and universal joy. Parties of women faced the famous star group and greeted it with song and dance." The appearance of Rigel inspired the same sort of rejoicing in northern New Zealand. The reported rivalry, of course, was not in the stars but in the calendar customs.

The festivals of South America are presumably quite unrelated to those of Polynesia, yet the Abipones and several other South American tribes used and personified the Pleiades just as the Maoris did. In both cultures the Pleiades gave the signal for a festival; in both they were saluted with joy, and, just as personification is implied when the poet addresses the West Wind or the city of Rome, when the drinker addresses his drink, or when the priest officiating at a moon-timed ceremony addresses the moon, personification is at least implied in the salutes addressed to the Pleiades. Songs and dramatic dances may have developed the myths, so that the stars became personified more specifically as ancestors, as ghosts honored at the dead-feast, or as a tribal god presiding over the New Year. "The task of Matariki," according to the Maoris, "is to keep moving in a cluster, to foretell fat and lean seasons, and bring food supplies to man." Some Maoris say that Matariki is one person, a female. Others say that the Pleiades are Matariki, a fe-

male ancestress, and her six children. Polynesians generally agree with the Abipones in making the little
constellation one person, a male who is sometimes an
ancestor. None of these personifications can be *seen* in
the stars. Like the notion of Rigel's hostility to the
Pleiades, they are inspired by the use of the stars to
define the beginning and end of the year.

The well-known Greek personification of the Pleiades
as nymphs pursued by Orion is more directly related to
the movements of the stars as they can be observed on
a clear autumn night. In the northern hemisphere Orion
rises after the Pleiades and appears to gain on them as
he "pursues" them from east to west. Another example
of a story inspired in part by the visible phenomena
comes from the Marshall Islands; there it is said that
two brothers competed in a canoe race for the kingship
of the heavens. The younger, called Jabro (the Pleiades)
beat his eldest brother Dumur (Antares) and thus became King of the Stars. These two parted in anger,
Antares vowing never to see his brother again. Consequently, when the Pleiades are visible, Antares is invisible. The Pleiades, here as elsewhere in the South
Seas, are "king" or "chief." The fact that Antares disappears before the Pleiades rise and reappears after their
setting can be observed by any watcher of the heavens;
the kingship is conferred by the calendar-maker.

Another personification makes each of the Pleiades a
dancer. For instance, a Cherokee star-myth tells how
seven youths dancing a feather dance were transformed
by the moon into the group of seven stars, and directed
"to dance for ten days each year over the Red Man's
council house; that being the season of his New Year.
One of the dancing brothers, however, hearing the
lamentations of his mother, looked backward; and im-

mediately he fell with such force that he was buried in the earth." The feather dance was performed regularly in honor of the Pleiades; it takes its name from the fact that each of the seven dancers held in his hand seven eagles' plumes of different colors. Stith Thompson, in his *Tales of the North American Indians,* says that versions of this story have been found among seventeen tribes, from the Tlingits in the extreme Northwest to the Yokuts of California and eastward to the Iroquois and Onondagas. The scattered versions of the story were presumably transmitted from tribe to tribe or handed down from the same original source. However, the personification of the Pleiades as dancers is not limited to the North American Indians. According to one Greek tradition the stars were the seven daughters of the Queen of the Amazons; they instituted choral dancing and nocturnal festivals. In Morocco and in India they have been called Dancing Maidens; to the Wyandot tribes of North America, also, the dancers were girls rather than boys. So many coincidences in the personification of the Pleiades suggest that some sort of explanation is in order.

When I say that no stargazer can discern the figure of an ancestor, a chief, or a "king of the stars" in the little cluster we call the Pleiades, I feel that I am on firm ground. If I say that the Pleiades do not look like dancing youths or maidens, I am contradicting those authors who have said that the arrangement of the Pleiades does suggest a group of dancers. However, my own view is that the observer must strain his imagination to *see* them as male or female, dancing or standing still. To the Australian Blackfellows, the Pleiades are the seven Maya-Mayi, girls who sing corroborees while their rejected suitors, the stars of Orion, dance. The Kiowa Indians, too, called them Singing Maidens; in Wyandot mythology they both sing and dance. The truth is that they do not look like dancers any more than they sound like singers. For an explanation of these coincidences in star tradition we must look further.

One mythologist who has paid some attention to the Pleiades, A. H. Krappe, has offered a suggestion. The stars are dancers, he says, because in tropical and sub-tropical zones the appearance of the Pleiades announces the rainy season. Since it is an almost universal custom to perform rain dances just before the beginning of the rainy season, these dances were synchronized with the rising of the Pleiades. The human dancers therefore looked upon the stars themselves as dancers, even, some-times, as divine beings who had originated the art and taught it to their countrymen. When he made this sug-gestion Dr. Krappe was, I think, getting warm, but I would go still further. Not all dances are rain dances; not all Pleiades dancer myths are tropical or subtrop-ical. Whenever a ceremonial dance of any kind is timed by the position of the Pleiades, the stars *may* then be-come personified in song or tale as dancers. This answer seems to me logical and satisfactory so far as it goes. The timing of the festival accounts for the Pleiades-ancestor myth as satisfactorily as it accounts for the Pleiades-dancer myth, but without forcing us to see in the ar-rangement of the stars the figure of an ancestor as well as a *corps de ballet*. Fortunately, we do not have to guess at the existence of ceremonies or festivals timed by the Pleiades; we have as much evidence for them as we have for the myths, and the evidence comes often, though not always, from the same cultures.

If Pleiades mythology is to be explained by festival customs, however, we must assume that regular obser-vation of the Pleiades preceded the assimilation of the ancestors or festival dancers to the stars. For instance, the constellation may have been observed with reference to the moon, especially the new and full moon, and also with reference to the dawn and dusk. Let me illustrate with a little story from Tahiti. In the year 1806 the London Missionaries were spending a quiet evening in prayer when they were suddenly interrupted by the excited shouts of the natives. The missionaries went out to investigate, and found that a new moon had appeared. For some months, says the report, there had been a dispute about the setting of the Pleiades. Some said the constellation would set or "fall, and go to bathe in the sea," before the death of the last moon, and others denied it. "These last were rejoicing, for now the moon had changed and the stars were still above the horizon." Interpreted, this story means that the Tahitians had been disputing whether or not this year was the year of thirteen moons. The "last moon" can only mean the twelfth moon; the new moon that caused the excitement would have been the thirteenth moon. Since it appeared before the evening setting of the Pleiades, the Tahitian year corresponding to our year 1806 must have had an intercalated month. Like most Polynesians, the Tahitians determined the end of one year and the beginning of the next by observation of the Pleiades. Also, like most people who use the sky for both clock and calendar, they probably timed the exact days of the New Year festival by the moon.

Or take another example, this time from Thailand, where the birthday festival of Karrtikeya lasted into this century. In the Indian astronomical tradition, the Pleiades are seven sisters called the Krittikas. The month of Karrtika, named for the Krittikas, is the month when the Pleiades accompany the full moon across the night

sky, rising at evening, setting at dawn. The story goes
that one time when the Krittikas went down to bathe
in the Ganges at dawn, they found the infant god
Karrtikeya drifting near the shore. They made a nest for
him in the reeds and became his foster mothers. In
Thailand his birthday was celebrated each year in the
month of Karrtika when the moon was nearest to the
constellation of the Pleiades.

The Pleiades look no more like the foster mothers of
Karrtikeya than their companions the Hyades look like
the foster mothers of Dionysus. This is one more example of star personification which is (surely in one
case and probably in both cases) related to calendar
usage and festival custom. Other examples of Pleiades
observation, collected by Sir James Frazer, can be found
tucked into a note following volume seven of *The
Golden Bough*. He mentions the "extravagant joy"
shown by many diverse people at the rising of the constellation. He tells how the Hottentot mothers carry children to the hilltops to "show to them those friendly
stars, and teach them to stretch their little hands towards
them." He remarks on the Bantus and Kaffirs of Africa,
the Blackfellows of Australia, the Paraguayans of South
America, Cherokee and Blackfoot Indians of North
America, and the Maoris of New Zealand, all of whom he
lists among those who observe, personify, or worship the
Pleiades. In some languages the word for Pleiades was
the same as the word for year; in other words, the
Pleiades, not the solstice, served as anchor for the calendar. They formed the peg from which the year depended.

The presumed origin of astronomical science in the
Fertile Crescent is occasionally mentioned in connection
with star mythology. We have some evidence that the

Pleiades were being observed, and their position recorded, as early as the third millennium B.C. in Mesopotamia. However, there seems to be no justification, let alone necessity, for assuming that the Hottentots, Blackfoot Indians, Abipones of the Gran Chaco, and Maoris all had their calendars from the Babylonians. The Pleiades are in everybody's sky, along with the moon. The fact that they have been used more often than any other asterism to determine a New Year's date may indicate that the traditions are related, although they are certainly not uniform. Some observe the morning rising, some the evening rising, some the evening setting.

The seasons marked by these phenomena vary, of course, according to the latitude of the observer; they have also varied through the millennia since men first took note of the sky. Whatever the season, if the Pleiades are observed as a time signal they may be credited with power over the crops, the weather, the availability of fish or game. So, the Maoris say, the Pleiades bring food supplies; in South America they were said to encourage the growth of manioc; in North America the Cherokees used to say that if the feather dance were not performed according to ancient usage, the Pleiades might send bad weather. This is another aspect of personification and another step on the way to divinity. These sayings, like the myths, are dependent upon previous observation of the Pleiades to mark the passing of time.

The observer who personifies a group of stars as several dancing girls may be poet as well as calendar-priest; but not even a poet would personify six stars as seven girls. It is much more reasonable to suppose that the tradition of the seven Pleiades originated when seven stars were clearly visible to the naked eye. We know that

stars do fade from view or grow brighter. The discovery
of a seventh Pleiad, lurking just out of sight but discern-
ible by means of a small telescope, justifies the assumption that the lost seventh star was once bright enough
to be counted with the other six. Stories that tell how
one star disappeared from the group confirm this view
beyond any reasonable doubt.

An early Greek work attributed to Hesiod, "The
Astronomy," names the seven sisters: "Teÿgeta, and
dark-faced Electra, and Alcyone, and bright Asterope,
and Celaeno, and Maia, and Merope." Hesiod (if he was
the author) obviously counts "dark-faced Electra" as the
invisible sister. The story goes that she was seduced by
Zeus, and bore him a son called Dardanus, ancestor of
the Trojan kings. Her disappearance was caused by her
grief over the fall of Troy and the extinction of the
Dardanian line. Other authors have made Merope the
missing Pleiad. After her marriage to Sisyphus she hid
her face in shame, being doubly disgraced: he was both
a mortal and a criminal.

It might be added that the Maoris, among others, say
that the seventh star is still visible, given perfect view-
ing conditions and perfect eyesight. The Australian
Blackfellows speak of seven Maya-Mayi, of whom *two*
are less brilliant than their fellows. All seven are of
course dark-faced, but they are said to be encased in
glittering ice. The relative dimness of two stars is explained by a story telling how those two were captured
while the seven sisters were on a visit to earth. The man
who captured and married both of them tried to thaw
the ice at his campfire, but they escaped and rejoined
their sisters before he had quite succeeded. With the
exception of one important detail—the capture of two
girls instead of one—the story from Australia corresponds

to the well-known American Indian tale of Algon and the Star Chief's daughters, who descended from the sky in a basket to dance on the prairie. Another step brings us full circle to the Wyandot Singing Maidens and so to the Cherokee feather dance. However, the story of Algon or Waupee is one variant of a famous folktale named from its central motif: "The Star Wife." Sometimes the star descends voluntarily to be wife to a mortal; sometimes she is captured when she descends with her sisters to bathe in the sea. Like the better known Swan Maiden she sometimes removes her garments or her wings, and her future husband captures her by stealing them.

Here we confront some of the most perplexing questions the mythologist has to deal with: Are folktales invented simply for entertainment's sake, passed from tribe to tribe, from culture to culture, and, here and there, adapted to religious uses, thus becoming myths? Do they well up from some deep psychological reservoir, taking the form of a myth in one culture and an Arabian Night's entertainment in another? Does the myth outlast its cultural use and so become a folktale? Is there any relation between the myth and the folktale? Is there any difference between them? The Star-Wife motif gives the daring mythologist a perfect opportunity to grapple with these questions if he wishes to do so. The Star-Wife folktale is grafted upon, crossed with, or merged into the Pleiades myths in more than one culture. When this happens, we can ask not only the general questions mentioned above, but specific ones: Did the tale of the star who married a mortal travel about the world as a tale whose heroine is an unidentified single star, perhaps a falling star? Did the star woman acquire sisters, become somehow crossed

with the Swan Maiden, finish as a Pleiad? Or did observations of the Pleiades, combined with the festival songs
and customs, give rise to the myth of the Pleiades as
dancing girls, one of whom was captured and married
a mortal?

My own view—and it is only a view, not a convic-
tion—is that the problem of personification lies somewhere near the heart of the matter. There are reasons,
with their roots in calendars, festivals, ritual dances and
New Year observances, why the Pleiades may be personified as one or several ancestors, or a bevy of dancing
maidens. When the Pleiades in the form of star maidens
are said to come to earth to dance and sing during one
season of the year, this is an extension of the personification. When seven unidentified star girls are said to
visit the earth once a year to bathe or wash their summer dresses, I hear an echo of the Pleiades myth. When
one is captured and disappears from the sky, I remember the missing Pleiad. When she marries a mortal and
becomes the ancestress of a tribe or clan or royal line,
nothing seems more natural, given the ceremonies and
mythology associated with the Pleiades. On the other
hand nothing seems less natural if we leave out of consideration the function of calendars and the traditional
uses of the stars. The psycho-symbolical schools of
myth interpretation, which might have been expected
to do something about a star wife, have pushed her to
one side with the other stars and star myths. The attitude of the comparative mythologist has, in fact, paralleled that of the astronomer: the star myth is a silly
story inspired by the configuration of the stars; it is not
really a myth in the sense that stories of the creation,
for instance, are myths; it is rather a folktale, a "why"

story, which may safely be left to the motif-indexer or collector of star names.

While this attitude has prevailed among the comparative mythologists, the field anthropologists have consistently recorded star myths as myths. In the broad study of a single culture the link between the star myth and the agricultural or liturgical calendar is usually apparent to the investigator who understands the first thing about time-telling. If the story is used as explanation for a festival, if it is enacted in a ceremonial dance, if the star personae are worshiped in prayer or addressed in song, the story deserves the mythologist's attention. A comparative study of star mythology would be helpful, but it should be correlated with a comparative study of calendars. In the case of the calendars the cross-cultural parallels are obviously not accidental; they have their roots in the universality of time measurement by the sun, moon, and stars. Of these three the stars are neither most nor least important; they are simply the third leg of a three-legged stool.

The man who collects several hundred versions of the Star-Wife tale is doing at least as much to help along the study of mythology as the man who analyzes the motivation of the star's kidnapper when he stole her clothes or digging stick. But the many variants of the Star Wife or the Pleiades myths are also incomplete in themselves. We need other data from the cultures that produced or transmitted them. Along with the California Indian story of the seven girls who rose into the sky on eagle-down ropes, to remain there as the Pleiades, we need to know that the man who wanted luck in gambling watched their heliacal rising through his own eagle-down talisman. Along with the story of the dancing boys, we need information about the feather dance and the Pleiades New Year. We need these facts just as much as we need to know what the maguey is and how it is used before we analyze the mythological role of the goddess Mayauel, the deity of the plant.

Finally, we should realize that a Star Maiden may have as good a right to the mythologist's attention as a Corn Maiden. When we read that the sisters of the six (sometimes seven) Corn Maidens of the Zuñis were Seven Maidens of the House of Stars, and, further, that among the same people corn kernels and stars were identified, we may even wonder which is which. A comparison of the Zuñi Corn-Maidens myth with the Star-Wife folk-tale and the Pleiades mythology is enough to convince one lay mythologist, at any rate, that agriculture has had the upper hand too long. The stars deserve another investigation, broader and deeper than any studies made in the past.

PART V

13) A view of the quarters

The importance of time and space concepts in the work of the Jung-oriented mythologists is a curious paradox. The symbolism of time and space is extensive and fascinating, but so far as I can see it contradicts in all its aspects the Jungian hypothesis of mythology as an emanation of the preconscious psyche. The quartered circle itself may be as important in psychoanalysis as Jung believed, but the symbolism and mythology of quartered time and space had to follow upon the conscious observation of the heavens. Using his eyes and his wits, putting two and two together, man learned to orient himself according to the cardinal points. Discovery of the four directions was an important step in the cultural history of the human race, and disorientation is a well-known symptom of mental illness, but if there is any relation between the one kind of orientation and the other kind of disorientation it must be exceedingly remote.

On the other hand, many contemporary students of mythology outside the Jungian influence are inclined to overlook or deny the effect of time and space observation on mythology. There is a prevailing notion that time and space concepts are too abstract for the mythmaker to comprehend. A consideration of the symbolism together with the phenomena that gave rise to that symbolism may help to correct both these misconceptions. The elementary problems of space division, starting from scratch, must have been solved by an observant, rational, wide-awake intelligence—in other words, by a man who could have fashioned the first boat from a hollow log, or made the first hand-axe out of a rough stone. Time and space problems were solved step by step, by people who must have been looking for answers to practical, even inevitable questions like "When?" and "Where?" I do not suggest that they were grappling with the riddle of the universe or deliberately setting about to fashion a cosmogony.

Nobody knows what people first quartered space, but I should suppose that they were preliterate, since space division is less difficult and more important to survival than the invention of writing. Once the technique of finding the cardinal points was mastered, it was cherished, used in ceremonies and handed down from generation to generation. The original symbolism (necessary to nonliterates who are handling the abstract concepts of east, west, north and south) was elaborated. The directions were personified, impersonated, deified. Above all, they were used; they were used by nomads, hunters, and the builders of the Egyptian pyramids. Prehistoric towns in both Europe and Asia were laid out on a grid-pattern with streets aligned to the four quarters. The dead were buried facing east or west, north or south. Perhaps graves were oriented because of superstitious beliefs concerning the quarters of space, but it is obvious that the quarters had to be determined before superstitions could become attached to them.

The fact that all men everywhere have chosen to divide the circle of the horizon into four primary directions tells us nothing about the human mind except that it can observe and make use of natural phenomena. The apparent movements of the sun, moon and stars caused by the earth's rotation dictate the division of space into quarters. There is no east, west, south or north except as the earth turns on its axis and the lights of heaven appear to move across the sky. Sunrise and sunset enable the observer to distinguish two of his four directions: east and west. The position of the sun at noon and the direction of the noonday shadow mark the other two: north and south. These facts may seem too obvious to be worth mentioning, but the first men to order their observations of moving light and shadow in a system of space division that was universally applicable were benefactors to their race.

Sun observation, however, is only half the story. By night the stars and moon confirm the observations made by daylight; they too rise in the east and set in the west. After dark the most conspicuous direction is north in the northern hemisphere, south in the southern hemisphere. Those are the directions of the stars that slowly wheel above the horizon and never set at all. In the southern hemisphere there is no star to mark the hub of the clock-

wise movement, but in the northern, the great constellation of the Big Dipper wheels counterclockwise around
the Pole Star, the only stationary light in the heavens.
Facing this star, a man has the rising on his right hand,
the setting on his left, and south, or noonday (*Midi,
Mezzogiorno,* as the French and Italians say) behind
him. Without these moving lights as guides, the only
directions would be local—upriver and downriver, towards and away from.

In a Pawnee creation story the sun and morning star
are placed in the east, the moon and evening star in
the west. The reason for these positions is, again, a matter of observation. Although *everything* rises in the east
and sets in the west, the new moon and evening star are
never actually seen in the eastern sky. They are seen
only in the western sky after sunset. Through the mil-
lenniums men have watched the western sky for the first
appearance of the new moon; therefore the moon, like
the evening star, is placed in the west by the Creator.
The morning star, on the other hand, is seen only in the
eastern sky before sunrise. Consequently it is associated
with the direction east. However, east is above all the
direction of dawn and sunrise, and so of the sun. These
associations are not peculiar to the Pawnees; they can
be duplicated in other mythologies because the phenomena are exactly the same, the world around.

Since the new moon and evening star both appear in
the west at sunset, and also because the sun sets in the
west, the direction west is identified with a time of day,
evening. Sunrise and the morning star cause the direction east to be identified with the hour of dawn. This
does not mean that the Navaho Indians, for instance,
could not distinguish between a direction and a time of
day. It means only that the same color served to denote

both morning and east, and the same deity ruled both the direction and the time of day. Noon, as we have already seen, is identified with the direction south in our latitudes because the sun, which rises in the northeast during the summer, will be south of the zenith by noon on every day of the year. That leaves us the identification of north with midnight, and in fact the Germans call the direction north *Mitternacht*. Again, every step in this coalescence of time and space symbolism is based on observation.

The next step, again based on observation, is the identification of the four seasons with the times of day and the directions. In a Pueblo Indian ceremony we are told that a certain goddess "makes alive from her basket the chiefs of Winter, Spring, Summer and Fall and sends them as Chiefs of the Directions to the Sacred Mountains" at the four cardinal points. Now the rising and setting of the sun and moon alone will not account for the identification of the horizon circle with that of the year. The identification is widespread and most important to time-space symbolism, but wherever it is found some observation of the fixed stars lies behind it.

Where no proof is possible, disagreements are of long standing, and no doubt they will continue to stand. "Early Man" (but it is not clear how early) is supposed by some authorities to have been incapable of noticing the fixed stars and distinguishing constellations. I disagree. I don't see how he could overlook them. When I say this, I am not arguing for a knowledge of the Zodiac, but only for the observation of three groups of stars: the Big Dipper and a pair of constellations that rose, one at dusk, one at dawn, when night and day were equal in length. The Dipper marked the north; the other two, which I shall call the Hare and the Hound, marked

the directions east and west with every rising and setting. Every night in the year, so long as there are no
clouds to obscure the sky, the rising or setting of one or
the other would be visible, and on most nights the patient observer can watch one set and the other rise, one
due west, the other due east, whereas the risings and
settings of sun, moon, and planets are constantly moving north and south along the horizon.

The constellations of the Hare and Hound, therefore,
are guides to the directions east and west; they are more
dependable guides than sunrise and sunset, and they
perform the same office in every part of the world.
Other constellations lying along the celestial equator
might have served the same purpose, but the Hare and
the Hound have a striking peculiarity. Whenever the
sun, the moon, Venus or any other planet rises due east
or sets due west, it will do so in the company of either
the Hare or the Hound. If the sun is rising and setting
with the Hare, only the Hound will be visible; he will
be visible all night long, and the night will be equal in
length to the day. If we suppose that the sun rises with
the Hare at the spring equinox, then the reverse will be
true at the autumn equinox: the Hare will rise at dusk
and set at dawn, while the Hound will be invisible.
Furthermore, the moon seems to have a special affinity
for these two constellations. So far as our hypothetical
Early Man is concerned, the sun keeps him warm and
gives him light, but the moon is more likely to arrest his
attention and cause him to think. If he watches the sky
at all, he is bound to notice her shifting phases and position. This is what he sees:

Once every month the moon runs all the way from
the southernmost point of her course to the northern-
most point and back again, constantly changing her

shape as she goes. (This is the same journey the sun makes in the course of a year.) Like the sun, the *full* moon will rise and set once a year in the company of the Hare, once with the Hound. Suppose she is in the company of the Hare at the autumn equinox: instead of rising about an hour later each night as she usually does, she will rise each evening for several successive evenings only about half an hour later, so that there will seem to be several nights in a row when the moon is at her full. This is what we call the Harvest Moon. Again, six months later, when the full moon is rising with the Hound, she reverses this singular performance, setting each morning for several mornings in succession near the hour of the sunrise. This is the full moon that marks the fluctuating date of Easter, and for convenience' sake I shall call it the Easter Moon.

The equinoctial constellations of the Hound and Hare could not be overlooked for long by any people who had learned to orient themselves by the four cardinal points; furthermore, the peculiar behavior of the moon at the equinoxes could not be overlooked for long by any people who used the equinoctial constellations as guide to the directions, especially if ceremonies even of the most rudimentary sort were timed by the full moon—as they so often are. The Hare and Hound, therefore, are identified not only with east and west but with the seasons when one is rising with the sun and the other with the *full* moon: that is, with the seasons of spring and autumn. The identification of spring, east, and sunrise follows so naturally that there seem to be no exceptions, or if there are, I have not found them. West, by the same token, is the direction of autumn and sunset. Here the time-space symbolism begins to be less uniform. In one tradition the Hare is the autumn constellation because it rises with the full moon of autumn; in another the Hare is the spring constellation because it rises with the sun at the spring equinox. Some identify south with winter, and others make it the direction of summer.

These variations are not whimsical: they are determined by the kind of calendar in use and the relative importance of solar and lunar observation. In the Zodiac we inherited from the Near East by way of the Greeks, the Hare was the constellation of spring, when it was invisible because it rose with the sun. In China, on the other hand, the same constellation was the constellation of autumn because at that season it dominated the night sky and was visible all night long.

The reader may object that we have no constellations called Hare and Hound. I suppose I must have written four or five versions of this chapter over a period of as many years before I realized that I had to invent my own names for these two constellations in order to explain the problems to the lay reader in their truly beautiful simplicity. For one thing, no two traditions agree in grouping the stars as constellations; the seven stars of the Big Dipper, the Pleiades, and the three bright stars of Orion's belt are among the exceptions. For another, the equinoctial constellations of four to six thousand years ago have moved to the north and south, and have become winter and summer rather than spring and fall constellations. To make these matters more confusing, the astronomers are using the name of the constellation Aries (the Hare of more than two thousand years ago) to denote that segment of the heavens where the constellation we call Pisces *now* travels, rising with the sun at the spring equinox. With the reader's permission, I shall continue to refer to the "Hare" and the "Hound." I am

otherwise forced to use circumlocutions like "the con-
stellation-that-was-rising-with-the-sun-at-the-spring-
equinox" every time I refer to one or the other. The conditions remain the same through the ages, but the stars
change.

At what point does a knowledge of the directions and
the association of two constellations with two seasons of
the year cease to be simply useful information and become part of one's mythological heritage? And how is
the transition accomplished? Presumably the transition
begins to take place as soon as the directions are used in
religious ceremonies. As for the reasons why they were
so used, I can think of several without being able to
prove one. For instance, the orientation of the sacred
ground where the ceremony is performed, together with
the repetition of gestures towards each of the four directions, serves to fix the four quarters in the minds of the
people, to instruct the young and preserve the tradition.
Furthermore, any ceremony is an overt act performed
in a prescribed manner. It must be done in the *right*
way, and the directions help to define a right way just
as the moon's phases help to define a right time. Also, in
a world without roads, maps and permanent buildings,
the orientation of the participants to the cardinal points
would provide a sense of stability: these are the four
guideposts of the universe, whose establishment was an
intellectual achievement to be remembered and cherished. The directions are next personified as gods, or
perhaps gods already in existence are assigned to each
of the four quarters.

A detailed discussion of the symbolism would run to
fifty pages before I had done more than scratch the
surface. Here I can only indicate the variety and at the
same time the consistency of the different traditions. In

the first place there are the four colors of the four quarters: they are found from Tibet to the American Southwest and Central America. No two neighboring tribes agree on the colors assigned to the directions; perhaps the differences are deliberate. The primary reason for assigning colors is presumably the need for a symbolism that will express the abstract concept of quartered space. Animals of the four quarters are scattered from ancient Egypt to ancient China and are well known in the New World. Again, the primary reason for assigning one animal to each direction would seem to be the need for a symbol that can stand for an abstraction. The colors suffice to distinguish the directions when the cosmogram is done in color like the Navaho sand-paintings; when the design is engraved on a bronze mirror, color alone will not serve. On the Chinese "cosmic mirrors" the animals are the Dragon of the East, Tiger of the West, Phoenix or Red Bird of the South, and the combined Tortoise-and-Serpent of the North. Dragon and Tiger were once, so we are told, the constellations dominating the spring and autumn skies. They are still members of the Chinese Zodiac. As spring and autumn constellations they became the animals of east and west as well. The Dragon, rising with the full moon (his pearl) at the spring equinox, was visible all night long: "When the Dragon has his pearl," the ancient Chinese writers said, "he does not sleep at all!" The color of east was green, and the Spring Dragon was a Green Dragon. The Tiger, symbol of the west (which was also signified by the color white), rose with the full moon at the autumn equinox. Since the Chinese celebrate their Moon Festival during the nights of the Harvest Moon, the White Tiger of the West became a lunar animal, and even a symbol of the moon herself

I find no suggestion that the "Four Intelligent Animals" of the Chinese tradition were deified, although they do occur in mythology, especially as companions to the Taoist goddess Hsi Wang Mu, Queen Mother of the West. The oldest attested *deities* of the directions are the Egyptian gods sometimes called the Sons of Horus. They were the Hawk-headed god of the West, the Ape-headed god of the North, the Man-headed god of the South, and the Jackal-headed god of the East. Impersonators of these gods are known to have played a part in coronation and funeral ceremonies of ancient Egypt. Canopic jars in sets of four, each with a stopper shaped to represent the head of one of the sons of Horus, were part of Egyptian grave furniture for at least two millennia. These jars held the entrails of the deceased, and were placed under the coffin containing the mummy.

The Maya Indians had four gods called Bacabs. Bishop Landa described them as "four brothers whom God placed at the four quarters of the world when He created it, supporting the sky so that it should not fall." If there were no more to the Bacabs than this, they would be hardly more than counterparts of the Norse dwarfs Ostri, Vestri, Suthri and Northri, who held up the sky at the four quarters. But the Bacabs again illustrate the coalescence of time and space in a single symbol. They served not only as four sky-posts at the cardinal points, but as the four cornerstones of the calendar. They were Year-Bearers, which is to say that they represented the four days which alone could serve as New Year's Day. The modern Mayas still identify the four mountains of East, West, South and North with the four cornerstone days of the calendar. The mountain is a god, the day is a god, and both are the same god.

The Maya calendar is so far removed from our conception of a proper calendar that I shall not attempt to describe it here. I shall only say that it is a brilliant astronomical and mathematical achievement, and definitely not the product of a preconscious psyche. I would also add that any study of the Bacabs based on psychological and anthropological theory without attention to the celestial movements and the Maya method of counting time is not only a waste of energy but downright misleading. When the Bacabs figure in a flood myth, the reasons must be sought in their roles as gods of time and space. When the Pleiades figure in mythology, the part they have played as Hare, the animal of East and Spring in some calendars, and of West and Autumn in others, should also be taken into consideration. Once upon a time, the Hare and Hound were tremendously important. They were important as facts everyone needed to know; they were important to religion, and they found their way into mythology from outside, not from inside.

14)   Space, time, and the flood myths

Flood myths, more than any other myths or mythological themes, have inspired and justified the comparative mythologist in his armchair pursuit of parallels. The Greeks had not just one tradition of a universal flood, but several reported from different parts of Greece. The Book of Genesis contains two fractured and spliced accounts. Archaeologists have disinterred two different cuneiform versions inscribed on clay tablets in two different languages. After the discovery of the New World, missionaries diligently recorded American Indian flood myths that seemed to them to corroborate the Old Testament account of the Deluge. Polynesia provided more parallels. In the early twentieth century Sir James Frazer made a comprehensive collection of myths, legends and folktales of devastating floods in his *Folklore of the Old Testament,* his aim being to demonstrate that flood myths from different parts of the world were not related; that they were not based on memories of one historical universal deluge; and that the story of the Flood in the Book of Genesis could not be accepted as a factual account.

Despite the two hundred and fifty pages Frazer devoted to his consideration of mythical and legendary floods, he left the real riddles unsolved. If the story of a universal deluge is not remembered history, why does it crop up in so many mythologies? Why do so many of the stories have certain minor details in common, although they differ radically in other ways? Why are flood myths found in so many cultures, from the poorest to the richest, but not in all? Frazer's negative approach, perhaps inevitable in his day, not only failed to answer these questions, but deliberately minimized the importance of the parallels. However, with the groundwork he provided, we should have been able to carry on, treating the myths as myths rather than history, and coming to some acceptable conclusion concerning their origin and wide distribution. But where are we? All at sixes and sevens.

Current mythological theories seem to me especially inadequate when they are applied to the flood myths. Lord Raglan, in *The Hero,* suggested that the flood myths probably originated in the great river valleys of the Nile, Euphrates, and Indus, where it was the duty of the king to ensure by ritual that the floods arrived punctually and were adequate to the agricultural needs of the people. The flood myths, according to this theory,

are descriptions of the flood-producing ritual. Perhaps;
but the difficulties remain.

Another attempt to swallow all the floods at one gulp,
as it were, is Mircea Eliade's assimilation of the flood
myths to aquatic symbolism in general; the Deluge is a
mythical counterpart to the act of baptism by total immersion. The sins of the world like the sins of the individual are metaphorically washed away. Lewis Spence
has offered a vague but comprehensive explanation in
which kingly rites and the purifying lustration of the
earth are combined. A flood story from Sumatra which
tells how the earth had become "old and shabby" and
was in need of renewal he finds especially significant.

Meantime, the biblical flood has again been taken
seriously as history. The distinguished archaeologist Sir
Leonard Woolley, digging near Ur of the Chaldees,
found evidence of a tremendous flood "of a magnitude
unparalleled in local history." He says: "Taking into consideration all the facts, there could be no doubt that the
flood of which we had thus found the only possible evidence was the Flood of Sumerian history and legend,
the Flood on which is based the story of Noah." After a
detailed description of his findings, he continues: "So
much for the facts. What, then, is to be built up on
them? The discovery that there was a real deluge to
which the Sumerian and the Hebrew stories of the
flood alike go back does not of course prove any single
detail in either of these stories. This deluge was not universal, but a local disaster confined to the lower valley
of the Tigris and Euphrates, affecting an area perhaps
400 miles long and 100 miles across; but for the occu-
pants of the valley that was the whole world!" As an
archaeologist, not a mythologist, he stops there and

leaves us to make what we will of the mythical details and corresponding flood myths found in other cultures.

Two obstacles hinder the mythologist who tries to deal with stories of flood. Although he is free, now, to assume that the biblical account is unhistorical, the tendency to take Noah's flood as the yardstick for his comparison, and to match other flood myths against it, still persists. Striking parallels in other traditions, but not in Genesis, are therefore likely to be obscured. A second obstacle is the difficult question of the diffusion of myths, in this case complicated by the possibility of missionary influence. The flood myths of the New World are fascinating, but they are open to question when they resemble the story of Noah and the Ark. The later they are, the more possibility there is that Noah has wormed his way into an aboriginal tale; the earlier they are, the more possibility that a missionary looking for corroboration of the biblical account has emphasized the coincidences. Perhaps the best way to avoid these obstacles is to put Noah and his animals into the bottom drawer— for the moment—and begin by looking at flood myths as far as possible removed from the Scriptural flood.

For a first choice, the story told by the Sia Indians of New Mexico has almost nothing in common with Noah's flood except the water. There was no rain; a flash flood appeared in the dry canyons and rose higher and higher until it was almost level with the tops of the mesas. As it rose, it obliterated the roads to the cardinal points. When Spider, looking to the four directions, saw that the road was obliterated, he cried, "Where shall my people go?" He then placed on top of the mesa a hollow reed through which his people could climb to the world above. Utset led the way, carrying a sack containing the stars. When they reached the upper (this) world, the sack was given into the care of the scarab beetle, who was ignorant of its contents. Out of curiosity, he cut a tiny peephole. Immediately "the Star people flew out and filled the heavens everywhere." He quickly grasped the sack and held it fast, but managed to save only a few of the stars. "Utset placed these in the heavens. In one group she placed seven—the Great Bear. In another three (Orion's belt?). In another group she placed the Pleiades, and threw the others far off into the sky."

The flood myth of the Sia Indians is clearly related to their creation myth, in which Spider establishes the directions. It is also related to the cosmology of other Indian tribes in the southwestern United States. There is, for instance, a similar story in which the Navahos tell how Coyote helped to place the stars following the ascent from the first world. We have many recorded versions of that ascent, most of them told as accompaniments to ritual sandpaintings in which the cosmology is depicted. Details vary, but the underlying pattern is the same. There have been four worlds, each denoted by a color, which is also the color of one of the four directions. This world is the fourth. At least one world, sometimes each of the first three, was destroyed by flood. The ancestors of the race emerged into the present world from the one below.

Farther south, among the Indians of the Middle American civilizations, the four quarters again play a part in the flood myths, this time through the gods of the four directions. Bishop Landa reported of the Mayas: "Among the multitudes of gods which this people worshipped, they adored four, each of which was called Bacab. They said that these were four brothers whom God placed at the four quarters of the world when He created it, supporting the sky so that it should not fall.

They said also of these Bacabs that they escaped when the world was destroyed by flood."

In the Quiché Maya story, found in the Book of Chilam Balam, the universal destruction was brought about by the four Bacabs themselves, who caused the heavens to be broken up and to fall upon the earth (in a flood). Kan-xib-yui was placed in the center "to order it anew." Four trees, each of a different color, were planted at the quarters, and a fifth at the center, each one symbolic of one destruction of the world. In an Aztec story, the four Sky-Bearers, when they had seen "that the heaven had fallen on the earth" ordained "that all four should make through the center of the earth four roads by which to enter it in order to raise the heavens . . ." This being done the gods Tezcatlipoca and Quetzalcoatl formed themselves into trees, and helped raise the heavens into place.

In still other Middle American traditions, the four worlds are associated with the calendar (time) rather than the directions (space). According to an Aztec account there were three previous worlds: the first was destroyed when a Jaguar devoured it on the day 4 Ocelot; the second was destroyed by hurricane on the day 4 Wind, the third by flood on the day 4 Water. The next will be destroyed by earthquake on the day 4 Motion. The modern Mayas of northern Yucatán subscribe to the four-world theory, but destroy each world by total immersion, a universal deluge.

The relation of each one of these traditions to all the others seems reasonably clear; whether the flood is one in a series of floods or the only flood in a series of world destructions according to a foreordained pattern, or a single flood wiping out an earlier world existing on a lower level, the interwoven themes are characteristically

Indian without the faintest overtone of the Biblical flood myth. If the New World flood myths just cited are to be compared with anything in the Old World, the nearer parallel is that tradition, familiar to the Greek and Roman writers, which held that there were to be four world ages determined by planetary conjunctions. The first had ended in universal flood during the Great Winter, when all the planets met in the Sign of Capricorn; another would end in fire when they met in Cancer at the summer solstice, and two other destructions would occur at the equinoxes, which were in turn associated with earth and air. The New World myths mentioned above might even be compared with a Hindu flood myth in which it is said that a universal deluge, marking the period of Brahma's nocturnal repose, occurs at the end of each long period called a Kalpa, or Day of Brahma. At such times, all the worlds up to the seven stars of the Dipper are submerged in the primeval ocean. When Brahma awakes, the world emerges from the sea and a new creation begins. The Eddic flood, which was foreordained to be the final act of a *Götterdämmerung,* comes nearer to these cyclic floods than to Noah's. The old earth was to be submerged in the sea and afterwards the resurrected Balder would rule over a new creation with a new generation of gods.

The most striking parallel in all these myths, the salient fact that emerges like Ararat from the flood waters, is that they are closely linked with creation myths; the flood wipes out the old creation and a new creation begins. In the more sophisticated versions, periodicity is explicitly stated.

The cyclic nature of the disaster in a number of flood myths has not escaped the notice of Eliade, who discusses the subject briefly in his *Myth of the Eternal*

Return. The recurrent floods are particularly appropriate to his theory of periodic cleansing and renewal. Both Eliade and Lord Raglan note the resemblance between flood myths and creation myths. In the greater number of creation stories the earth emerges muddily from primeval waters, and as it emerges a second (or third or fourth) time from flood waters, the creation is in a sense being repeated. In the "Earth-Diver" tales of some North American Indians the creation and the flood are so far confounded that it is difficult to tell which is which.

So far as creation myths are concerned, I am in accord with the Jungian interpretation which holds that many (but not all) are a setting-in-order of the universe. They define the divisions of time and space. Roads are drawn to the four directions; sun, moon and stars are set in the sky to tell time. When the creation is erased and made new, the directions are again established and time takes a fresh start. This much is fairly obvious, but the reasons for the destruction and re-creation are not at all clear. It seems to me that when Eliade emphasizes the cleansing of the earth, he is unduly influenced by the biblical flood myth in which an angry God is moved to destroy a degenerate race. Spence leans even more heavily on the sins and violated taboos which make necessary a symbolic lustration of the fields in order that the crops may grow. But the periodic floods described above come when it is *time* for an old order to be wiped out and a new one established.

If the New World myths I have mentioned belong to a common family, as seems probable, a pre-Columbian painting in the Dresden Codex offers a clue to all of them. In that document the Maya calendar-priests computed their long numerical cycles, and correlated them with planetary and eclipse cycles. On the last page there is a striking watercolor painting of a Maya cataclysm. Across the top of the page lies the body of a serpentine sky-monster, his side ornamented with symbols of the constellations. Blue water is cascading from his open mouth, and also from the signs of lunar and solar eclipses hanging from his banded belly. Two deities are shown in the lower part of the picture: Ek Chuah, a black warrior who sometimes wears the mask of the Pole Star god, and the moon-goddess Ixchel of the thirteen skeins of colored thread. She wears a knotted serpent in her headdress. A Moan bird (owl) of evil omen perches on Ek Chuah's head. Ixchel holds a jar from which she empties still more water containing the Maya sign for zero, or "completion." We have no text to explain the picture, but none seems to be necessary since it is self-explanatory. Each known symbol points to the same interpretation: this is the end of a great cycle, astronomically determined, fated to end in flood. Here missionary influence is impossible, and even the most ardent diffusionist would be hard put to find a link between the Maya conception and Woolley's Chaldean flood.

The Maya Indians, who were obsessed with time and time counts, may well have invented the theme of the cyclic flood and handed it on to their neighbors. There is no reason to suppose that they must themselves have acquired it at second hand, and less reason to suppose that they exported it as far as India and Greece. Any people with a creation story and a related calendar (sun, moon and stars created and set in the sky to tell time) might conceive of a cycle larger than the annual cycle, in other words, of a New Year's Day beginning a new creation. The parallels between the Maya symbolism and the corresponding Old World traditions of periodic floods, either European or Asiatic, can be explained by a parallel use of calendars and the presence of a time mythology related to them. Although the long cycles sometimes end in fire, sometimes in whirlwind or earthquake, water in some form seems to be the favorite means of terminating a world age. Perhaps one reason for the preference is that primeval ocean from which, in so many stories of the creation, the earth originally emerges. Since the world is to be created anew, it is temporarily submerged in water, and the second creation proceeds along the lines of the first.

Besides the cyclic cataclysms, which are patently linked to time and space concepts, there are North American folktales of a flood whose only survivor was the trickster hero of tribal mythology. Are we to suppose that the flood myths of Middle America sent out ripples as far as the Plains Indians, who adapted the theme to their own purposes in the trickster tales? This is, of course, possible. Coyote has a role in both types of tale; and when four animals figure as survivors in the Earth-Diver stories, they recall the four Bacabs. The Earth-Diver, however, can also be considered as an outermost ripple of another tradition originating on the Asiatic continent.

The situation is this: the Earth-Diver is an animal or bird that dives to the bottom of the flood waters (or, in creation stories, the primeval sea) to bring up a bit of mud from which the earth may be created or re-established. At first glance, nothing would appear to be more completely aboriginal than this theme; yet the Earth-Diver motif occurs in the same context among the Samoyeds of Siberia, where the folklorists consider it to be related to the American Indian tradition. It is also found in India, where Viśnu in his *avatara* as Boar brings up earth from the ocean depths for the same purpose. Diffusion of the Earth-Diver episode to or from India, Siberia, or North America is possible, even probable, but not proven. The trail is further confused by the account of the Babylonian tradition as given by Berossus, writing in Greek in the third century B.C. Birds figure in his story, as they do in the Hebrew and cuneiform versions, but instead of bringing back a leafy twig they returned to the Ark with muddy feet; this signified to Xisuthrus that the flood waters were retreating. In the Babylonian myth, however, there is no question of re-creation of the earth.

Murky as the problem of the Earth-Diver may remain, there is this to be said about the stories in which the earth is re-created or repopulated by miraculous means: these floods are not historical. Frazer indulged in a bit of hilarity at the expense of those mythmakers who did not have the prudence to make the survivor take along a wife and children so that the earth might be repopulated in a natural manner. Coyote in one story had to stick into the ground feathers which became living men and women. In another story he had to sing shaman songs to bring to life the bones of the drowned. Other survivors carved people from wood, made new men from bones that had been picked by eagles, and so on. The survivor in a Hindu myth produced a wife miraculously from the clarified butter of his postdiluvial sacrifice. Yet, as Frazer observed, even when a man and wife do survive, they may be instructed to repopulate the earth at once by extraordinary means. Deucalion and Pyrrha, who survived the flood that ended the Bronze Age, are a conspicuous example: they threw over their shoulders stones that became living men and women. In the early nineteenth century Indians along the Orinoco were telling similar stories of the earth's repopulation after flood.

Whether they had already come under classical influence is not known, just as we do not know the possible
influence of the Biblical story on, say, the Mandan Indian rite witnessed by George Catlin about the same
time. In some ways the Mandan story, which Frazer
gives in detail, is closer to the cuneiform myth than to
the version told by missionaries. The sole survivor,
Nu-mohk-muck-a-nah, was said to be still living in a
mountain in the West. Once a year a mummer, magnifi-
cently garbed in white wolf skins and a raven headdress, impersonated the Mandan Noah in ceremonies
commemorating the Great Flood. Going from hut to hut
in the village, he told to each inhabitant the story of the
flood and his own survival. So, in the story found at
Nineveh, Utnapishtim, who was the sole survivor, lived
on forever in a mountain to the East, and there he told
his own story to the Babylonian hero Gilgamesh.

Throughout this discussion, and in my title, I have
been careful to speak of flood myths in the plural. So far
as I have been able to discover, we are not justified in
speaking of "the flood myth" as though there were a
single prototype from which all the known versions developed. Nevertheless, the broad mythical theme of a
destruction of the world by water is commoner than we
should expect it to be, even when we allow for the fact
that the missionaries and explorers from Europe were
especially assiduous in collecting all the flood stories
they could find. The examples given above illustrate
something of the variety and something of the homo-
geneity encountered in a comprehensive collection of
flood myths.

As we saw earlier, the explanations offered for the
origin of the theme are three: historical, psychological

and ritual. No one of these is generally accepted. In this matter I can only speak for myself and emphasize that my conclusions are tentative.

The historical solution falls into two parts. The first, or fundamentalist, answer that there *was* one actual universal deluge seems to me untenable. If someone can prove that there was such a flood all our questions are answered. The other possibility is that there was one local, historical flood such as Sir Leonard Woolley described, and that the story of this flood with its mythical embellishments was distributed, presumably along with other stories and certain civilizing techniques, quite around the world. I should agree that all mythical floods are historical in so far as they usually take the form best known locally; for instance, a flash flood in the American southwest, a tidal wave in Polynesia, and so on. I should also agree that stories of a universal deluge have traveled long distances as part of a tradition, or different traditions; but my view is that these stories always were fables except for the descriptive details taken from experience of real floods. So far as world-wide diffusion of the theme is concerned, the flood myths must be considered in association with other stories having more or less the same distribution. This matter is much too complex to handle here.

As for the psychological answer, in the present state of our knowledge nothing can be proven for or against it. However, even if we accept purification symbolism as the ultimate origin of the flood myths, we must, I think, allow for diffusion of the myths without diffusion of the associated symbolism. All in all, the symbolist answer seems to me too far-fetched to entertain seriously.

This leaves ritual; and in the case of the flood myth I

should be inclined to accept a ritualist answer if I could find a suitable ritual. The agricultural rituals suggested by Lord Raglan and Lewis Spence raise the same sort of problem raised by both the historical and psychological answers. We should have to presume first a local origin where certain conditions obtained; then the diffusion of the story to peoples living under completely different conditions; and, finally, perpetuation of the myth in nonagricultural societies where it must have had another meaning entirely—providing, of course, that it had any meaning at all.

My suggestion is that we look first for meaning where it is easily found: that is, in those stories where the floods allow for—or account for—some adjustment of the creation, of space, of time, of heavenly or earthly dynasties. Perhaps a psychological need gives rise to the theme; but there is also the possibility that practical matters have forced the occasion. For some reason the old story and New Year ritual of the creation must be changed; a new ritual takes care of the changeover and in turn becomes a myth. Wherever the calendar or the legend of dynastic origins is interlocked with the creation story, a rearrangement may be needed. The stars do not abide forever in the same position; the social order is not static; a new beginning may be superimposed on the old. In more sophisticated versions where the calendar is involved, other beginnings may be forecast. Periodic erasure by water, which rises seasonally in the rivers, twice daily in the tides, would seem to be a natural means of destruction without the presence of symbolism. A story of this kind might originate more than once and in societies on different material levels of culture. It is portable; it can be carried as a story, and a very good story, until it meets another similar fable coming from another direction and one borrows details from the other. Any theory which leaves out migration of flood myths is in my view as surely inadequate as the theory which would trace all flood myths to their origin in one historical flood.

15) The sibling sucklings

In Italy twin boys were set afloat on the Tiber; discovered and suckled by a wolf, they grew up to found
the City of Rome. In Burma twin boys were hatched
from eggs floating on a stream; they were found and
suckled by a deer, and eventually became gods. The
twin Dioscures of Greece were also hatched from an
egg; and the twin creator-gods of the Cahuillas were
hatched from two eggs. According to the Zuñi Indians,
their twin culture-heroes were born from a dead mother
and adopted by a badger whose wife suckled them; the
badger made them bows and arrows and badger dresses;
they fought monsters and led the way to the upper
world. In Melanesia, twin boys were born of a dead

mother and suckled by a qena root; their adoptive father
(the trickster god Qatu) made them bows and arrows;
they killed a monster and avenged their mother. In
South America twin boys, culture heroes of Brazilian
mythology, were born to different fathers and adopted
by jaguars after the death of their mother; they had
many adventures; one died and was brought to life by
the other. In Siberia the twin boys Altin Shagoy and
Mungun Shagoy, or Gold Knee Cap and Silver Knee
Cap, were also exposed, adopted, had bows and arrows
made for them by a foster father, killed a monster, and
resurrected their own father, using the water of life.

The above summary, which might be extended by
several pages, presents several pretty problems. First,
there is the distinction between myth and folktale. The
Siberian story is a folktale. The characters are prodigious
but not divine; the story was not told to explain the
ceremonies or customs of the Koryaks who told it. Three
others are myths. The Burmese twins take possession of
mediums on festival days, and sing their own histories.
In the American Southwest and throughout much of
Brazil the hero twins are protagonists in the myths of
tribal origin. The Melanesian story is close to the border
line; Qatu, the uncle and foster father of the twins, is a
creator as well as a trickster god, yet one authority states
that the tales about him are not true myths, but only
"why" stories. In Homer the Dioscures are human
heroes, but a cult of the Dioscures makes it clear that
they sometimes shared their father's divinity. The Cahuilla twins are gods or culture heroes. The twin Aświns
of India are among the earliest twin heroes known, and
they also rank as gods. On the other hand the very
earliest tale of two brothers, a story which contains one
striking motif of the twin heroes mythology, has some

earmarks of a folktale and some kinship with the myth of Isis and Osiris; it comes from Egypt *circa* 1400 B.C. The Egyptian story is not about the gods, but about wonder-working men, and it is surprisingly similar to certain modern folktales on the same theme. We might say then that the theme is not *per se* mythical, but fits into either of two categories with equal ease.

The next problem, and the major one, is the question of the relationship between these sibling pairs. Do they come from a common ancestor, or not? The answers so far given have made a pendulum swing from yes to no and back towards yes, again, but with reservations. Obviously, it doesn't really matter, and nobody would waste time on the problem if it were not for the contrasting pictures of the human mind presented by the two contradictory answers. If the answer is no, we have to assume that the minds (conscious or unconscious) of the most diverse people have time and again projected the same images, the same plots, the same personae, even the same personae attached to the same plots. We must, if we accept the negative answer, come to the conclusion that the human mind is cut to a predictable pattern; once we pin down the archetypal outlines we should have the key to living. On the other hand, if a simple tale about twin brothers has traveled throughout Europe, Asia, the South Seas and both Americas, and has been employed as a myth again and again for lack of a better story, or any other story, we must conclude that the human mind is a singularly blank expanse. The imagination, far from being well stocked with energetic archetypes, is an inert organism awaiting a stray morsel of food.

For all its complications, the problem of distribution is much simpler in the case of the twins than in that of the flood myths. For one thing, the historical answer has never been favored by any writer; no one pair of twin heroes is supposed to have impressed itself upon the imaginations of men scattered over several continents. For another, missionary influence has not been at work. The twin heroes are found in classical literature, but not in the Bible. Cain and Abel resemble the twins described above only in so far as they are male siblings.

We have five remaining possibilities: independent origin in each case; independent origin in several cases with diffusion of the theme in a limited area; migration of the theme as a story passed from one group to another; migration of peoples carrying the myth with them; and, finally, a combination of two or more of the foregoing possibilities, as for instance independent origin of the twin gods and migration of plot details.

To begin with the first possibility, perhaps no one has actually held that each pair of twin heroes was invented independently. In South America, for example, the twin myths of the Urubus, the Teneteharas and the Tupinambas are in accord even to minor details, although the myths of the last-named tribe were recorded four hundred years before the others. Relationship therefore seems to be well established among neighboring tribes in Brazil. The Mayas also had a pair of mythical twins, or rather two pairs, but here the relationship with Brazil is not established. The same may be said for the Zuñis and Cahuillas. If we assume that the Greek, Roman, Hindu, and Melanesian twins originated independently, we may as well assume the same for the Zuñi, Maya and Tupinamba. This would bring us to the second possibility—multiple origin, perhaps even simultaneous invention with diffusion through a limited area from one tribe to another. But why the coincidence? A primal pair hatching from an egg that appeared in the void would make better sense if the two were male and female. Why should we have the repeated myth of two orphaned boys (usually twins) who are adopted by an animal and grow up to be gods or culture heroes?

Efforts have been made to answer this question. About a century ago D. G. Brinton wrote a passage in which he commented on the striking similarities between two pairs of twin heroes, one Asiatic, one American. "Such uniformity," he said, "points not to a common source in history, but in psychology." Brinton would have it, however, that the pairs were contrasted Light and Darkness contending for mastery, and that the mother was Dawn personified. Brinton's theories of nature symbolism were out of fashion almost before he had published his book. It was no longer good form to look for the psychological parallels in a similar reaction to a similar environment, specifically in a parallel personification of natural forces. Instead, the mythologists were turning to the study of parallel superstitions in search of answers. They found that a number of savage tribes had a superstitious fear of twins, and, to be brief about it, exposed them or killed them along with their unfortunate mothers. Those who survived, being outcasts, were supposed to have founded towns to which other renegades and outcasts repaired; eventually the twins who founded the community became heroes or demigods to their descendants. Frazer apparently accepted this theory. A. H. Krappe, who also accepts it, says in his discussion of the Heavenly Twins: "The twins, feared and persecuted as they were, enjoyed at the same time the signal honor of deification!" The punctuation is his own. One can't complain that the theory is absurd; the retort would undoubtedly be that the primitive mind deals in absurdities. Sometimes

I suspect the scholar's mind of dealing in greater absurdities. Let us say, simply, that the case for the emer-
gence of twin mythology from the superstitious fear of
twins is not proven. No other psychological explanation
for the pre-eminence of the twin heroes has, so far as I
know, even been suggested.

We cannot, simply for lack of a satisfactory explanation, abandon the possibility of independent invention
entirely. However, before I say more about it, I should
like to go on to the other possibilities. Theories of the
migration of peoples are always controversial, and for a
long time the migration of myths or mythical themes was
almost as unpopular with established scholars, although
both types of theory have attracted enthusiasts among
laymen and maverick anthropologists. Gradually, the
scholars have moderated their position to a point where
they now say that relationship should not be assumed (as
for instance between the Hindu and the Maya twin heroes) unless contact can be shown. There are American-
ists, however, who would be willing to grant that contact
is possible and even probable for all of both Americas;
and, further, that the traditions of some American Indian
and some Siberian tribes are surely related. Once we are
on the Asiatic continent there is considerable evidence
for contact between the Siberian traditions and the
Hindu, and ample evidence of exchange between Burma
and India. The possibility that the ancient Hindu and ancient Greek twins had a common parentage has often
been discussed. And in that case, why exclude Rome? The
further possibility, then, that the twin heroes have actually migrated most of the way around the world is not
so outlandish as at first it might seem. The trouble is that
we next have to ask ourselves why the twins, of all
people, should have had this marvelous endurance and

mobility, a question almost as hard to answer as the other question left dangling above. Are we to fall back on psychology again to explain the popularity of the twin heroes, and if so what answer can it give us?

Another difficulty presents itself: if the twin heroes entered the Americas by way of the Bering Straits and worked their way south, they must surely have done so at an early period. We have no evidence, so far as I have discovered, for an early tradition in Siberia. The folktales were recorded in the nineteenth century, whereas the twin myth of the Tupinambas was first set down in the sixteenth. The possibility of diffusion across the Pacific may yet turn out to be the more reasonable answer.

In the Introduction to *Dahomean Narrative*, the Herskovitses write: "Why the factor of diffusion has not been faced is due to the preoccupation of many students with the myths of peoples whose cultures are no longer living, or with the application of principles, theoretically derived, as they are held to relate myth to contemporary literature. The broad comparative view has in both cases been lacking." I suspect that the factor of diffusion has not been faced, first, because it is so damnably complicated, and second, because it threatens to undermine all principles, theoretically derived, concerning the origin, nature and function of myths. Suppose, for example, that we were actually able to encompass and overcome all the difficulties in our way, to trace the twin heroes in a long journey from Mesopotamia or India to Siberia and finally to the Amazon; suppose we discovered, then, that the twins had arrived by chance, stayed by chance, and moved outward partly by chance, and partly for lack of competition. Mythology is not studied for itself; it is studied because the pattern in the carpet is supposed to

tell us something; but what if we were to find that the
pattern is accidental and tells us nothing at all? Heaven
forbid.

Lord Raglan, in *The Hero,* supported the diffusionist
view chiefly on the grounds that an illiterate people is
incapable of invention. The argument was so preposter-
ous that it invalidated the whole discussion. Some illiterate people invented writing, a noteworthy step in the
history of civilization. And if illiterates can invent writing they can also invent myths; in fact, they have. Furthermore, as the anthropologists have often pointed out,
there is no reason why anything that has been invented
once should not have been invented more than once. If
one set of mythmakers has combined a pair of orphaned
twins with a few popular folklore motifs such as the
abandoned or floating infant, suckling by animals, a
dragon fight and eventual apotheosis, there is no reason
why twenty other groups should not do the same. The
odds are against it, however, unless a still undiscovered
pattern in the carpet actually exists.

The odds are not so heavily against the independent
invention of twin deities in several different cultures.
Subsequent borrowings of plot details, in that case,
would not be especially surprising. A pair of indigenous
brothers might well attract to themselves stories told of
a foreign pair who resembled them. This is the fifth
possibility and the one to which I am most inclined. The
fact that the brothers may in one or both cases have
divine stature does not count against the free assimilation of new incidents to a cycle of myths already in
existence. The Egyptian story of Isis as a foster mother
is an almost exact parallel to the Greek story of Demeter and the infant Triptolemus or Demophoön. The
theme of the child cradled in the fire was probably bor-

rowed by one mythology from the other; and if the Greeks or Egyptians could borrow their myths, so might the Zuñis. It is to be noted that, although the plot was borrowed, there is no evidence that the goddess of whom the story was told was not herself wholly indigenous.

In his discussion of the theme, Krappe follows Rendel Harris in referring to the twin heroes as the "Heavenly Twins," an epithet they have earned in some cases by their origin, but more often by the fate that befalls them in the end, when they are removed to the skies. The Greek twins became the constellation of the Gemini; the Aświns of India married the sun; the Zuñi twins ascended to their Sun Father, as did the Navaho; the Maya twins Hunahpu and Xbalanque went to the skies where one was given the sun and the other the moon; in Brazil and the Gran Chaco there is a tendency to associate them with sun and moon, or sometimes with stars in east and west; in Tonga they became the Magellanic clouds; in two tales, one from South America and one from North Borneo, the brothers mount to the sky through a magical or shamanistic performance. These parallels raise difficulties of a slightly different sort. The eventual translation to the skies may be looked upon as an incident belonging to the core of the myth, or as an incident assimilated to the plot independently in different cultures, or, if we accept the fifth hypothesis mentioned above (independent origin of the twins and migration of plot) as an incident belonging not so much to the plot as to the twin heroes in their original manifestations as gods or demigods identified with, say, sun and moon, dawn and dusk, or east and west. In that case Brinton would be at least half right. For those who insist that nature symbolism in mythology does not exist, I would point out that in these cases it *does* exist. How-

ever, we do not know whether the association with the
sun and moon had anything to do with the origin of the
myth, or whether the twins, already full blown and with
their myth complete, were finally identified with the
heavenly bodies.

To quote the Herskovitses again, they speak of the
"classical evolutionists who, at the turn of the century,
followed the logic of their position, holding that re-
semblances in mythologies even of peoples living not too
far apart were to be accounted for by similar reactions
to similar environments. For reasons that are not ger-
mane to the discussion here, the position of the classical
evolutionists had been refuted many years ago. But certainly no better explanation has been offered since by
students of mythology." I do not count myself a classical
evolutionist, nor yet a nature mythologist if we mean by
that term the school of thought which found mythical
origins in "the need of early man to explain the movements of the heavenly bodies." I do hold that mythologies go hand in hand with certain cultural phenomena,
for instance, ceremonies, festivals, rites for the dead, the
shaman's performance as healer or medium. For practical reasons having to do with calendars and orientation, the sun, moon, stars, quarters and even years and
days have been personified. Once personified, there is
no reason why they cannot acquire a mythology, and so
in fact they do.

So far as the sun and moon are concerned, the more
usual form of personification is that of brother and
sister or husband and wife. Twin brothers are more
likely to be assigned to the directions, especially east
and west, or to the equinoctial constellations marking
east and west. But sun and moon, or morning star and
evening star, or dawn and dusk, may be assigned to

East and West respectively, in an elaboration of space symbolism.

A nature mythologist would go on from here to relate the incidents of the plot to the personifications, but I see no need to do so. The adoption by animals, the dragon fight, the search for the father's or the mother's bones, resurrection of one by the other, could migrate as separate episodes from culture to culture and adhere to twin heroes wherever they were to be found. The motifs of the floating infant, the miraculous suckling, and the dragon fight have perhaps adhered more often to the single hero.

Inevitably, I can give no more than a personal view of what is reasonable or unreasonable; here it is, for whatever it is worth:

It is not reasonable to suppose that each pair of twin heroes originated independently, and that all the parallels, including incidents of the plot, just happened. Currents of migration must have been at work, although these may have been migration of motifs rather than peoples.

It is not reasonable to suppose that any people simply borrowed its gods ready-made from another man's folktale. The borrowings must have been rather in the form of costumes, props, accessories, and incidental dramatic action.

Invention of twin gods two or three times is possible and plausible; limited diffusion would probably account for the others. The gods themselves may have been carried on some current still undetected. Shamanism offers a possibility, but that is a subject for another study.

CONCLUSION

CONCLUSION

16)   The mythmakers

In the foregoing chapters I have raised more questions
than I can hope to answer. The unanswered questions
are not only inevitable in the present state of our knowledge, but essential to an understanding of the subject.
My intention has been, not to set up a system, but to
examine a few themes, to find out what light they shed
on mythmaking in general. I have not even attempted
a definition of the word "myth." I now have a confes-
sion to make: I sometimes doubt that there is such a
thing as a myth. If myths really exist, I reason, there
should be an adequate definition somewhere, but I have
failed to find it. And if there are no myths, is there such
a thing as myth? Friends who know more about phi-

losophy than I do assure me that this is possible. However, before we deal with that monster, myth, a word more about myths.

There is something to be learned from the simple fact that no enlightened university has established a Chair of Mythology. Mythology is not a field in itself, but a patchwork of the corners of other fields. The chair would have to be a bench long enough to seat students of literature, linguistics, religion, archaeology, anthropology, psychology (two or three schools), folklore and philosophy. Besides that we need a stool somewhere for the poet. Mythology is seldom studied for itself alone, but only as it throws light on some other study. Definitions vary according to the interest of the scholar. They emphasize subject matter, function in "primitive" society and modern society, function in literature, origin (presumed), relation to religion, distinction from theology, and so on. Very well, what is a myth?

One thing I have learned during these years of study is that a myth under close scrutiny tends to change its spots or fade away entirely. Detach it from its fellows, from its associations with religious cult and social custom, and it rapidly dries out, loses its mythic juices and blows away in the first sigh exhaled by the mythologist.

On the other hand, any tale, whether myth or not, when brought into juxtaposition with a system of psychological symbolism, immediately acquires spots and turns into a myth. Herein lies much of the confusion current about mythology. More confusion lies in the broad use of the term "myth" to denote almost any concept (especially those which are demonstrably untrue) or the content of any poem, play or novel.

The popular conception of a myth is a useful starting point for a definition. The lay reader who is only casually interested in the subject will probably describe a myth as a story about gods and goddesses; questioned further, he would say, no, of course the story is not true, because the gods and goddesses don't exist. How could a story about Apollo be true? Questioned still further, he would probably agree that the story, although untrue, was believed by the people who told it. Confronted with the story of Hathor, he would reason in this way: the Egyptians worshiped Hathor, therefore they believed in her; she would not have been a goddess had they not believed; and those who believe in a goddess will believe also the stories told about the goddess. An admittedly untrue tale about a deity would be blasphemy. But would the mythmaker himself (who was possibly a priest) be one of the believers? Did he look upon the story as divine revelation? At this point my hypothetical reader bogs down. Mythology never interested him very much anyway.

Most anthropologists, I believe, turn their backs on questions of origin and limit their discussion to the function of a myth in the society where we find it. The Herskovitses define a myth simply as "a narrative which gives symbolic expression to a system of relationships between man and the universe in which he finds himself." If we accept this definition, we may suppose that the mythmaker need not have believed the story except as a symbolic expression of the relationship between himself and the festival beer, a small but important part of his universe.

The questions of truth, untruth, degree and kind of belief are perhaps the most difficult involved in the definition of a myth. Although not every myth concerns the actions of gods and goddesses, most readers would expect a myth to contain elements of the fantastic, impossible or miraculous, and I have accepted this distinction, not without doubts. The story I told in my first chapter about the accidental invention of beer by the Toba Indians seems to me almost a myth, although it lacks the element of the unbelievable. Perhaps to the Indians who told it fermentation *was* miraculous. The popular use of the word "myth" outside the study of mythology would indicate that a narrative, to qualify as a myth, must be believed. Barton, writing of the Ifugaos, defines myths "by the criteria of credence and function." But credence is hard to come at in some cases. I prefer to admit, besides the traditional stories of deities, any tale that is used by a society in association with its rites, religious exercises, festival dances, or ceremonies. Some people probably believe it, and some don't. A myth is not necessarily dogma.

There are further difficulties, however, when a tale not directly associated with religion or social custom appears to be a survival from an earlier time when it may have served as a myth. Shall we be rigorously correct and leave it out of the discussion, or shall we include it on the chance that it formerly qualified as a myth? A similar difficulty arises in the comparison of themes from different cultures. I have mentioned this point before, but let me give another example:

Apollodorus tells the Cretan story of Glaucos, who died in a pot of honey. Daedalus, having seen a serpent bring its mate to life with a magic herb, was able to resurrect the dead boy by the use of the same herb. Now some stories of resurrection are myths, and some (by the definitions discussed above) are not. This one apparently is not. However, Nonnus tells a precisely similar story from Asia Minor, and here, although we know almost nothing of the religious customs, we do

know that the city of Sardis represented the resurrected
hero on its coins along with his savior, the serpent, and
the magic herb. This would hardly have been the case
if the story had been no more to the Lydians than an
amusing tale. Both these serpents, furthermore, have
been compared to the serpent that stole the herb of life
from Gilgamesh in the Babylonian epic. This ancient
serpent has managed to slither under the wire and into
the fold, perhaps partly because the herb of life episode
in the Gilgamesh epic follows the story of the Deluge,
which is easily identified as a myth. The whole epic,
however, is described as secular, and in no way related
to religious rites and ceremonies. What shall we do? If
we call one serpent story a myth, one a doubtful case,
and one simply an entertaining tale, there is still the
probability that all three were once the same thing,
either myth or folktale. In China another story of a
serpent that brings its mate to life with a magic herb is
associated with a festival: it is performed on the day of
the festival, and one episode in the story is directly related to the festival customs. Nevertheless, it sounds to
the Western ear more like a fairy tale than a myth. Most
Chinese myths do, for that matter. I should like sometime to try to find out why.

The herb of life is balanced by the water of life,
which is used to resurrect the goddess Inanna in the
famous story of her descent through the seven gates of
hell. A water of life with precisely the same properties
occurs in a number of myths and many folktales. For
instance, it is used to resurrect the father of the twins
in a twin tale collected in Siberia. Here, one story of
the resurrection is apparently a myth, and the other apparently is not, yet we may want to compare them. What
do we do then? For the most part, we get around the

difficulty by speaking, not of myths, but of "myth," a word whose use I have avoided from the first page to the last chapter because I distrust it. Of course it can be useful; we can bundle everything into it—the three Weirds, Hathor as the Eye of Re, dragons, moon superstitions and ceremonies, folklore and fairy tale, and, now, Moby Dick and the Great Gatsby. But I submit that if we bundle too much into it, it ceases to be of any use whatever.

Myth is experienced subjectively and usually written about subjectively also. A definition of myth by Alan Watts will illustrate what I mean: "Myth is to be defined as a complex of stories—some no doubt fact, and some fantasy—which, for various reasons, human beings regard as demonstrations of the inner meaning of the universe and of human life." When I ask myself, "*Which* human beings?" the first answer that comes to mind is, "Alan Watts." Few or none of the individual stories I have discussed in the foregoing chapters are "demonstrations of the inner meaning of the universe" to me or to the people who told them originally. Or so I believe. Are they for that reason to be excluded from the "complex" of stories called myth? Complex: "A whole made up of complicated or interrelated parts," according to the dictionary. A wood, made up of trees; but the wood is something more than a collection of trees: it is experienced as a whole; its shadows, smells, footpaths, animal tracks, bird calls, and a ruined mossgrown hut at the heart of the wood are all part of the experience. Mr. Watts and others, having entered the wood, have come back to tell us that it is haunted, but I wonder.

Stith Thompson has complained that "most of the

authors who have written about myth make very little effort to connect their work with such myths as one actually finds when he reads collections from all parts of the world." The author of a subjective description entitled "A Walk in the Woods," seldom pauses for an exhaustive examination of the individual trees. But my metaphor is inexact because trees are not man made, whereas every myth was created by the mind of man. Furthermore, the mind was not floating free in a void, as myth tends to do. If we study myths as myths, not myth, we come back again and again to the problem of the mythmakers, who they were and what they were doing.

Most definitions of a myth add to the other requirements a stipulation that it must be traditional. That is, it must have become traditional by the time we first catch sight of it. This means, of course, that we can never see a mythmaker in action. If we do, he is not making a myth, but a song, a story, a dance, or a dramatic production, perhaps a ritual. Or are the mythmakers not the originators of the tale, but the almost equally invisible succeeding generations who have passed it along until by some process it became a myth? There is something in this; if the story of Oedipus is a myth, first Sophocles and later Freud helped to make it one. But are there not some tales that are myths from the beginning, perhaps even before they became traditional? Do others begin as folktales, being later adapted to religious or communal uses? Where and when does a myth begin to be a myth?

At every point in our definition a door stands open to let "myths" wander in and out. None of the doors will lock.

Whatever their ultimate origin, all the myths we know were either written down in ancient times or collected from oral sources in comparatively modern times. When we have parallel myths from both sources there is no way to prove that the oral tale was not handed down from ancient, literate cultures. This leaves an opening for the assumption that all myth (that complex described above) is an inheritance from those ancient civilizations, or, more likely, from a mythopoeic age when all myths were oral, an age earlier than the earliest civilization, when the ancient myths originated among preliterate peoples. Myth, in that case, is a heritage, conscious or unconscious, from prehistoric ancestors.

Now while it is true that we can never catch sight of a mythmaker in action, there are times when we can *almost* do so. In a previous chapter I mentioned the Tamyush of the Luiseños of California. The Tamyush was one of the personae of Luiseño mythology as well as a stone mortar in which jimsonweed was crushed and mixed. The Luiseños adopted the jimsonweed cult after the white men arrived, and it died out within about fifty years. At one point in their ceremonies these Indians raised a chant: "The Tamyush walks by twisting!" And so it did, being moved from side to side as well as forward, like a barrel being moved in an upright position. We find the Tamyush in mythology, therefore, walking down the road leaving a snakelike trail in the dust. This is not much of a myth, to be sure, but it is at least the beginning of a myth originating among a preliterate people. We do not find it among neighboring Diegueños and others who also used the toloache. It certainly does not go back to predynastic Egypt or Mesopotamia, nor is it borrowed from any literate society of modern times. It is unique, although the Tamyush as a person can be compared to the Norse cauldron Odrörir, which was also a person.

As myths developed, plot must also have been discovered and developed. I find myself thinking of "good" myths, by which I mean myths with a suspenseful story line or good dramatic action. A search provides one of the best plots, with its elements of repetition and suspense: Demeter's search for her daughter, the bee's search for the honey of immortality in the *Kalevala,* the search for Telipinu in the Hittite myth, the search for the water of life in the Sumerian story of Inanna. The pacification of an angry deity—Hathor or the Japanese Amaterasu or Telipinu again—also suggests a good plot. To raise one final question, how much of any "good" myth is there simply for the sake of the plot?

When I think of the earliest mythmakers, I think of them as much like the Luiseños, raising chants over their drinking bowls, and inadvertently germinating the first myths. Whether any of those myths have actually come down to us is another question. I doubt it. Sometime, somewhere, the earliest myths we know also originated. I imagine the mythmakers as living for the most part out of doors. I suppose them to have engaged in singing, dancing, and drinking as well as in agriculture and hunting. They took care of birth and death in suitable fashion, and handed down ceremonies from generation to generation. They made festivals, not necessarily agricultural, and hung them on calendars fashioned for the purpose. Since myths are usually held in common by all the people, I imagine myths as originating especially at those times and in those places where people come together for ceremony and festival.

Readers of *Middlemarch* will remember the Reverend Mr. Casaubon, whose great work, a *Key to All Mythol-*

ogies, dragged on for decades and finally remained unfinished at his death. One reason for his difficulties, no doubt, lay in the fact that there is no such thing as a passkey that will unlock every myth. Let the reader make up his own key ring. If I have helped him to make a selection, I am satisfied.

NOTES

1) HOW TO MAKE A MYTHOMORPH.

p.   4   *Mayauel:* Gonçalves de Lima, *passim.*
p.   4   *pulque-making:* Toor, 15–17.
p.   5   *Jung:* in Jung and Kerenyi, 101.
p.   7   *soma:* Hopkins, 112–24; Bouquet, 88–89; MacDonnell, 105–108; Hastings, article "Vedic Religion."
p.   8   *Toba Indians:* Métraux (1946), 54–56.
p. 10   *Abipones:* Dobrizhoffer, 435.
p. 10   *Urubus:* F. Huxley, 109–10.
p. 11   *kava:* Williamson (1939), 53–112, 273–78; Handy, 322; Christian, 187–92.
p. 12   *Kvasir:* Snorri, 93–95; MacCulloch (1930), 26, 53; Krappe (1928), 53–70.
        general: Driver, 266–70; Mackenzie, 53–80; Hastings, articles "Drinks and Drinking," and "Sacraments."

2) THE GOD IN THE FLOWERPOT

p. 14   *peyote, general:* La Barre, *passim;* Driver, 270 ff.
p. 14   *peyote, Huichol and Tarahumara:* Toor, 251–61.
p. 15   *mescal beans:* Troike, *passim.*

p. 17 *peyote myths:* Petrullo, 34–41; Stenberg, 139.
p. 19 *jimsonweed:* Gayton, *passim.*
p. 19 for *kava* and *soma,* see notes to chapter 1. For *awa:* Beckwith, 94–95.
p. 19 *mushrooms:* Wasson (both refs.) *passim.*
p. 20 *quinine:* Maddox, 249–52.
p. 22 *"There is no better way":* Wasson, vol. ii, 293.
p. 23 *Huxley, A.:* 21.
p. 23 *"The mushrooms sharpen":* Wasson *(Life),* 118–20.
p. 23 *"Le llevan": ibid.,* 114.
p. 24 *Li Po:* Bynner and Kiang, 63, 254 n. 34a.
general: Lewin (both refs.) *passim;* Eliade (1951), *passim.*

3) MOON MYTHOLOGY RECONSIDERED.

p. 26 *Krappe:* (1930), 205.
p. 27 *moon ceremonies:* Webster, 142–43.
p. 30 *Thoth:* Hooke, 28–30.
p. 30 *Nannar:* Webster, 226.
p. 30 *Mamaquilla:* Mason, 204.
p. 31 *Eliade:* (1958), 174–75; see also Bendann, 124–25.
p. 32 *Frazer:* (1924), vol. i, 65–67.
p. 32 *soma:* see notes for chapter 1.
p. 32 *Briffault:* vol. ii, 631.
p. 34 *Cora Indians:* J. E. Thompson (1939), 144.

4) THE MYTHMAKER AS ACTOR.

p. 39 *Cahuilla:* Hooper, 317 ff., 330–31.
p. 42 *Chadwick:* 93–94.
p. 42 *Czaplicka:* 240–42.
p. 43 *Frazer:* (1919 FOT), 542–44.
p. 44 *Duwamish:* Waterman (1930), *passim.*
p. 44 *Singapore:* Elliott, 137–40.
p. 45 *Miaos:* Graham, 73.
p. 46 *shaman's ascent:* Czaplicka, 237–38.
p. 46 *Tlingit:* Krause, 198–99.
p. 48 *Joseph Campbell:* 258.
p. 49 *Levi-Strauss:* in Sebeok, 52.

5) TO MAKE THE GODS LAUGH.

p. 56 *Uzume:* Anesaki, 226–27; Ridgeway, 302–303.
p. 56 *Hathor:* Sachs, 91.
p. 56 *Prose Edda:* Snorri, 91–92.
p. 57 *Radin:* p. ix.
p. 57 *Kerenyi:* in Radin, 174.
p. 58 *Jung:* in Radin, 196.
p. 59 *Loki:* MacCulloch (1930), 142.
p. 59 *Rahu:* see chapter 11 and notes.
p. 60 *Welsford:* (1927), 258–59.

6) A DRAGON HUNT.

p. 63 *Tiamat:* Langdon, 294–302.
p. 63 *Maya dragon:* see chapter 14 and note.
p. 64 *la Tarasque:* Porte, *passim.*
p. 65 *Kohler, Wolfgang:* Sachs, 10–11.
p. 65 *Sahagun:* Sachs, 153.
p. 66 *symbolic combats:* Gaster, 31–35.
p. 67 *Celtic dragons:* Jackson, 158–62; MacCulloch (1918), 200.
p. 67 *Chinese dragon and pearl:* Saussure, 354.
p. 67 *Illuyankas:* Gurney, 180–83.
p. 68 *eight-headed dragon:* Nihongi, 52–53.
p. 68 *St. Margaret:* Baring-Gould, viii, 485–87.

7) WHO WAS HATHOR?

p. 73 *Hathor:* Larousse, article "Hathor"; Baikie, *passim.* Budge, vol. i, p. xxvii; Muller, 37 ff.
p. 75 *"enjoyed immense popularity":* Larousse, *loc. cit.*
p. 77 *Mayauel:* see chapter 1, and notes.
p. 78 *Wilson:* in Pritchard, 10–11.
p. 79 *red coloring matter:* this is Wilson's explanation of the *tataat.* Anthes omits mention of it.
p. 79 *Anthes:* in Kramer (1961), 18.
p. 81 *"the symbol of the Archetypal Feminine":* Neumann, 221.

8) THE SOOTHSAYERS.

p. 83 *weird sisters:* MacCulloch, 246.
p. 84 *Voluspo:* Bellows, 1–27.
p. 84 *Chase:* 86–87.
p. 86 *MacCulloch:* (1930), 246–47.
p. 87 *Neumann:* 294–95.
p. 87 *Graves:* Index, under Cauldron.
p. 88 *Kvasir:* see chapter 1, and note.
p. 88 *Tamyush:* DuBois, 77–79, 156.
p. 88 *Leland:* 9.

9) GRANDFATHER PLEIADES AND OTHER ANCESTORS.

p. 95 *Frazer:* (1919 SCW), 308.
p. 95 *Dobrizhoffer:* 64–66, 91–94.
p. 95 *South Americans and Pleiades ancestors:* Métraux (1946), 23; F. Huxley, 209–10.
p. 96 *Pukapuka:* Beaglehole, 375–77, 309.

10) SECOND THOUGHTS ON EGG SYMBOLISM.

p. 100 *Eliade:* (1958), 414.
p. 101 *Easter Island egg hunt:* Métraux (1940), 331–41; (1957), 130–39.
p. 103 *palolo:* Agassiz, 16.
p. 104 *Eliade: loc. cit.*
p. 105 *Day of the Swallow's Return:* Granet, 158.
p. 105 *Chien-ti:* Waley, 275; Bulling, 122–23.
p. 105 *Maori:* Dixon, 20–21.
p. 106 *Kalevala:* Runo I.
p. 106 *Mahabharata:* Nott, 2.
p. 106 *Society Islands:* Dixon, 20.
p. 106 *Hawaii:* Dixon, 20.

11) ECLIPSE.

p. 110 *Mang woman and sweeper-god:* Penzer, vol. ii, 82.
p. 111 *ceremonial bathing:* Spier, 326.

p. 111   *offering to moon:* Krause, 185.
p. 111   *toad and eclipse:* Maspero, 40.
p. 111   *Todas:* Rivers, 592–93.
p. 113   *Urubus:* F. Huxley, 41–42
p. 114   *Moon Girls and Sun Boys:* Maspero, 40.
p. 114   *husband and wife:* Maspero, 40; Alexander (1916), 257.
p. 114   *brother and sister:* Weyer, 383–84.
p. 114   *Shakespeare: Hamlet,* Act I, Sc. 1.
p. 114   *moon is sick:* DuBois, 164.
p. 114   *Pachamac:* Dobrizhoffer, 85.
p. 114   *arrow-shooting:* Bett, 18; Granet, 233; Frazer (1958), 90.
p. 115   *Mangaia:* Makemson, 173; Gill, 47.
p. 115   *eclipse demon is a star:* Métraux (1928), 51.
p. 115   *Bagobo:* L. Benedict, 245.
p. 115   *Rahu:* Dumézil, 5–7.
p. 116   *dog and pestle:* Htin Aung, 145–48.
pp. 116–117   *eclipses studied in China:* Needham, vol. iii, 244 note a, 409–10.
p. 117   *South America:* Métraux (1946), 33.
p. 117   *Fenris-wolf:* MacCulloch (1930), 199–200.
p. 117   *Aztecs:* Vaillant, 195.

12) THE DANCING STARS.

p. 121   *heliacal:* once a year each of the stars in the Zodiac becomes invisible as it rises in daylight; the first visible rising after this annual period of invisibility is called the heliacal rising.
p. 121   *Maori:* Best, 25–27, 43–44.
p. 121   *Abipones:* see chapter 9, and notes; also Métraux (1946), 23.
p. 122   *Marshall Islands:* (1924), 72–73.
p. 122   *Antares:* a Scorpionis. Cf. the Greek myth of Orion and the Scorpion.
p. 122   *Cherokee:* the quotation is from Alexander (1916), 26–27.
p. 123   *Morocco:* Hagar, 360.
p. 123   *India:* Noble and Coomaraswamy, 387.
p. 123   *Maya-Mayi:* Parker, 105–109; Dixon, 294–96.
p. 123   *Kiowa:* Hagar, 254–56.
p. 123   *Wyandot:* Barbeau, 316–18.
p. 124   *Krappe:* (1938), 337–42.
p. 125   *London Missionaries:* Williamson (1933), vol. i, 172.
p. 125   *Karrtikeya:* Moor, 52–53.
p. 126   *Hyades:* a "later legend" according to the *Oxford Classical Dictionary.*

p. 126   *Frazer:* (1919 SCW), 307 ff.
p. 126   *word for year:* Breasted, 58.
p. 127   *manioc:* Métraux (1928), 51.
p. 127   *bad weather:* Hagar, 359.
p. 129   *Algon or Waupee:* Hagar, 360; Schoolcraft, 31–33.
p. 131   *eagle-down ropes:* Gayton and Newman, 50.
p. 132   *Corn Maidens and Star Maidens:* R. Benedict, vol. i, 271, 276, 325; Judson, 117–118.

13)   A VIEW OF THE QUARTERS.

p. 135   *Jung:* for a discussion of the mandala and the cardinal points, see Kerenyi's remarks in Jung and Kerenyi, 21–24.
p. 138   *Pawnee creation story:* Alexander (1916), 108.
p. 139   *Pueblo Indian ceremony:* Parsons vol. i, 246.
p. 141   *"the equinoctial constellations . . . have moved":* for an explanation of this phenomenon see "Precession of the Equinoxes" in any handbook of astronomy.
p. 144   *cosmic mirrors:* Cammann, *passim.*
p. 144   *Chinese constellations of Dragon and Tiger:* Saussure, 162–63, 377.
p. 144   *Dragon and pearl: ibid.,* 354.
p. 145   *Sons of Horus:* Fairman, 78–79; Tirard 19–24.
p. 145   *Bacabs:* J. E. Thompson (1934), *passim.*
p. 145   *Norse dwarfs of the directions:* MacCulloch, 264–65.

14)   SPACE, TIME AND THE FLOOD MYTHS.

p. 148   *Frazer:* (1919 FOT), vol. i, 104 ff.
p. 148   *Lord Raglan:* 145–46.
p. 149   *Mircea Eliade:* (1954), 63.
p. 149   *Lewis Spence:* (1961), 75–79.
p. 149   *Leonard* Woolley: 23–24.
p. 150   *Sia Indians:* Judson, 64–67.
p. 151   *Coyote places stars:* King, 13–14.
p. 151   *Navaho creation and migration myths:* Finegan, 50.
p. 151   *Bishop Landa:* J. E. Thompson (1934), 211.
p. 151   *Sky Bearers: ibid.,* 216–17.
p. 152   *Quiché Maya:* Alexander (1920), 154.
p. 152   *Aztec:* Spinden, 358.
p. 152   *Modern Maya:* Morley, 190.
p. 152   *flood and planetary conjunctions:* Eliade (1954), 87–88.

p. 153   *Hindu flood:* Frazer (1919 FOT), vol. i, 183–93.
p. 153   *Götterdämmerung:* MacCulloch (1930), 338–47.
p. 153   *Eliade and cyclic floods:* Eliade (1954), 63, 72, 87–88, 122.
p. 154   *pre-Columbian painting:* Morley, 188.
p. 156   *Earth-Diver:* Armstrong, 65, 89–90; Alexander (1916), 299–300.
p. 156   *Viśnu:* Hastings, article "Deluge."
p. 157   *Xisuthrus:* Frazer (1919 FOT), vol i, 107–108.
p. 157   *Orinoco:* Brett, 386. These Indians threw over their shoulders the fruits of the Maurita palm, from the kernels of which sprang men and women.
p. 158   *Mandan rites:* Frazer (1919 FOT), vol i, 294.
p. 158   *Utnapishtim: ibid.,* 112–18; Kramer (1956).
         general: Frazer (119 FOT), vol i, 104–361; Hastings, articles "Deluge" and "Ages of the World."

15) THE SIBLING SUCKLINGS.

p. 162   *Burmese twins:* there are two pairs, Nats XIII and XIV, and Nats XXV and XXVI. Scott, 348–53; Ridgeway, 252–53.
p. 162   *Cahuilla twins:* see chapter 4 and notes (Hooper).
p. 162   *Zuñi twins:* R. Benedict, vol. ii, 43–52.
p. 162   *Melanesian twins:* Codrington, 398–402.
p. 162   *Brazilian twins:* Métraux (1928), 31–41; F. Huxley, 217–25; Wagley and Galvao, 137–40. See also Nimuendaju on the Tukuna brothers, 134; and Hastings, article "Twins" for Keri and Kame of the Bakairi tribe.
p. 162   *Siberian twins:* Curtin, 222–31.
p. 163   *Hindu twins:* Hopkins, 81–84; MacDonnell, 49–54.
p. 163   *Egyptian story of two brothers:* Rugoff, 200–208; Pritchard, 23–25.
p. 165   *Maya twins:* Popol Vuh, *passim.*
p. 166   *Brinton,* 205–206.
p. 166   *Frazer:* (1924), vol. iii, 24.
p. 166   *Krappe:* (1930), 209.
p. 168   *Herskovits:* (1958), 84–85.
p. 169   *Lord Raglan: passim.*
p. 169   *Isis:* Plutarch, paragraphs 15–16.
p. 170   *Tonga:* Gifford, 103–109.
p. 170   *South America:* Métraux (1928), 206.
p. 170   *North Borneo:* Evans, 149–50.
p. 171   *Herskovits:* (1958), 84.
         general: J. Rendel Harris, both refs., *passim.*

16) THE MYTHMAKERS.

p. 177   *Herskovits:* 81.
p. 178   *Barton,* 4.
p. 178   *Apollodorus:* III, iii, 1.
p. 178   *Nonnus:* Frazer (1906), 98–99.
p. 179   *Gilgamesh:* Sandars, 114.
p. 179   *China:* Dols, 248–49.
p. 179   *Inanna:* Kramer (1944), 86–98.
p. 179   *twin tale:* Curtin, 292–300.
p. 180   *Watts:* 7.
p. 180   *S. Thompson:* in Sebeok, 104.
p. 182   *Tamyush:* DuBois, 77–79, 156.

BIBLIOGRAPHY

Agassiz, Alexander. "The Islands and Coral Reefs of Fiji." In the *Bulletin of the Museum of Comparative Zoology*. Harvard University. vol. 33. 1899.

Alexander, Hartley Burr. *North American Mythology*. Boston, 1916.

———. *Latin American Mythology*. Boston, 1920.

Anesaki, Masaharu. *Japanese Mythology*. Boston, 1928.

Apollodorus. *The Library*. Loeb ed.

Armstrong, Edward A. *The Folklore of Birds*. Boston, 1959.

Baikie, James. *Egyptian Antiquities in the Nile Valley*. New York, 1932.

Barbeau, C. M. *Huron and Wyandot Mythology in Canada*. Dept. of Mines, Geological Survey. Memoir 80. No. 11 Anthropological Series. Ottawa, 1915.

Baring-Gould, S. *The Lives of the Saints*. New and Revised Edition. Edinburgh, 1914.

Barton, Roy Franklin. "The Mythology of the Ifugaos." *Memoirs of the American Folklore Society*. vol. 46. Philadelphia, 1955.

Beaglehole, Ernest and Pearl. *Ethnology of Pukapuka.* Bishop Museum Bulletin 150. Honolulu, 1938.

Beckwith, Martha. *Hawaiian Mythology.* New Haven, 1940.

Bellows, Henry Adams, ed. and tr. *The Poetic Edda.* Princeton, N. J., 1936.

Bendann, E. *Death Customs.* New York, 1930.

Benedict, Laura Watson. *A Study of Bagobo Ceremonial Magic and Myth.* Repr. from the *Annals* of the N. Y. Academy of Sciences. vol. xxv. pp. 1–308. May 15, 1916.

Benedict, Ruth. *Zuñi Mythology.* 2 vols. New York, 1935.

Best, Elsdon. *The Astronomical Knowledge of the Maori.* Wellington, 1922.

Bett, Henry. *Nursery Rhymes and Tales.* New York, 1924.

Bouquet, A. C. *Sacred Books of the World.* Penguin ed. 1954.

Breasted, J. H. *Time and Its Mysteries.* Collier Books ed. 1962.

Brett, William Henry. *The Indian Tribes of Guiana.* London, 1868.

Briffault, Robert. *The Mothers.* 3 vols. London and New York, 1927.

Brinton, Daniel G. *The Myths of the New World.* 3rd ed. rev. Philadelpia, 1905.

Budge, E. Wallis. *Egyptian Literature.* London, 1912.

Bulling, Anneliese. *The Meaning of China's Most Ancient Art.* Leyden, 1951.

Bynner, Witter, and Kiang Kang-Hu. *The Jade Mountain.* New York, 1951.

Cammann, Schuyler. "Types of Symbols in Chinese Art." *Studies in Chinese Thought,* ed. Arthur F. Wright. Chicago, 1953.

Campbell, Joseph. *The Masks of God: Primitive Mythology.* New York, 1959.

Chadwick, Nora K. "Shamanism Among the Tatars of Central Asia." *The Journal of the Royal Anthropological Institute of Great Britain and Ireland.* vol. 66, 1936. pp. 75–112.

Chase, Richard. *Quest for Myth.* Baton Rouge, 1949.

Christian, Frederick William. *The Caroline Islands.* London, 1899.

Codrington, R. H. *The Melanesians.* New Haven, 1957.

Cole, Fay-Cooper. *Traditions of the Tinguian.* Field Museum of Natural History: Pubn. 180. Anthropological Series. vol. xiv. no. 1. Chicago, 1915.

Curtin, Jeremiah. *A Journey in Southern Siberia.* Boston, 1909.

Czaplicka, M. A. *Aboriginal Siberia.* Oxford, 1914.

Dixon, Roland B. *Oceanic Mythology.* Boston, 1916.

Dobrizhoffer, Martin. *An Account of the Abipones.* Tr. Sara Coleridge. 3 vols. London, 1822.

Dols, Father P. J. "Fêtes et usages pendant le courant d'une année dans la province de Kan-sou (Chine)." In *Annali Lateranensi.*

Publicazione del Pontificio Museo Missionario Etnologico, vol. 1. Città del Vaticano, 1937.

Driver, H. E. *Comparative Studies of North American Indians.* American Philosophical Society Transactions. n.s., vol. 47, part 2. 1957.

DuBois, Constance Goddard. "Religion of the Luiseño Indians of Southern California." *University of California Publications in American Anthropology and Ethnology.* vol. 8, no. 3. Berkeley, 1908–10.

Dumézil, Georges. *Le festin d'immortalité.* Annale du Musée Guimet, Bibliothèque d'Études 34. Paris, 1924.

Eliade, Mircea. *Le chamanisme et les techniques archaïques de l'extase.* Paris, 1951.

———. *The Myth of the Eternal Return.* Tr. Willard R. Trask. New York, 1954.

———. *Patterns in Comparative Religion.* Tr. R. Sheed. New York, 1958.

Elliott, Alan J. A. *Chinese Spirit-Medium Cults in Singapore.* London School of Economics and Political Science. Monographs on Social Anthropology no. 14, n.s., 1955.

Evans, Ivor H. N. *Studies in Religion, Folklore and Custom in British North Borneo and the Malay Peninsula.* Cambridge (Eng.), 1923.

Fairman, H. W. "The Kingship Rituals of Egypt." In *Myth, Ritual, and Kingship,* ed. S. H. Hooke. Oxford, 1958.

Ferguson, John C. *Chinese Mythology.* Boston, 1928.

Finegan, Jack. *The Archaeology of World Religions.* Princeton, 1952.

Frazer, Sir James G. *Adonis, Attis, Osiris.* London, 1906.

———. *Folklore in the Old Testament.* 3 vols. London, 1919.

———. *Spirits of the Corn and of the Wild.* 2 vols. London, 1919.

———. *The Belief in Immortality.* 3 vols. London, 1924.

———. *The Golden Bough.* 1 vol. ed. New York, 1958.

Gaster, Theodor H. *New Year.* New York, 1955.

Gayton, Anna Hadwick. *The Narcotic Plant Datura in Aboriginal American Culture.* Ph.D. thesis. University of California, 1928.

——— and Newman, Stanley S., *Yokuts and Western Mono Myths.* Anthropological Records, University of California. vol. 5, no. 1, 1940.

Gifford, Edward Winslow. *Tongan Myths and Tales.* Bernice P. Bishop Museum Bulletin. 8. Bayard Dominick Expedition Publication no. 8. Honolulu, 1924.

——— and Block, G. H. *California Indian Nights Entertainments.* Glendale, 1930.

Gill, William Wyatt. *Myths and Songs from the South Pacific*. London, 1876.

Gonçalves de Lima, Oswaldo. *El maguey y el pulque en los codices mexicanos*. Mexico-Buenos Aires, 1956.

Graham, David Crockett. *Songs and Stories of the Ch'uan Miao*. Smithsonian Miscellaneous Collections. vol. 123, no. 1. Washington, D.C., 1954.

Granet, Marcel. *Danses et légendes de la Chine ancienne*. 2 vols. Paris, 1926.

Graves, Robert. *The White Goddess*. New York, 1948.

Groot, J. J. M. de. *Les fêtes annuellement célébrées à Emoi*. Annales du Musée Guimet, tome 12. 2 vols. Paris, 1886.

Gurney, O. R. *The Hittites*. Penguin ed. 1952.

Hagar, Stansbury. "Cherokee Star-Lore." *Boas Anniversary Volume of Anthropological Papers*. pp. 354–356. New York, 1906.

Handy, E. S. Craighill. *Polynesian Religion*. Bishop Museum Bulletin, no. 34. Honolulu, 1927.

Harris, J. Rendel. *The Cult of the Heavenly Twins*. Cambridge (Eng.), 1906.

Harris, J. Rendel. *Boanerges*. Cambridge (Eng.), 1913.

Hastings, James, ed. *Encyclopedia of Religion and Ethics*. New York, 1908.

Herskovits, Melville J. and Frances S. *An Outline of Dahomean Religious Belief*. American Anthropological Society Memoirs, vol. 41. Menasha, Wis., 1933.

———. *Dahomean Narrative*. Evanston, Ill., 1958.

Hooke, S. H. *New Year's Day*. New York, 1928.

Hooper, Lucile. "The Cahuilla Indians." *University of California Publications in American Archaeology and Ethnology*. vol. 16, no. 6. Berkeley, April 1920.

Hopkins, Edward Washburn. *The Religions of India*. Boston and New York, 1895.

Htin Aung, Maung. *Burmese Folktales*. Calcutta, 1948.

Huxley, Aldous. *The Doors of Perception*. New York, 1954.

Huxley, Francis. *Affable Savages*. New York, 1957.

Jackson, Kenneth Hurlstone, ed. and tr. *A Celtic Miscellany*. Cambridge, Mass., 1951.

Judson, Katharine Berry, ed. *Myths and Legends of California and the Old Southwest*. Chicago, 1912.

Jung, C. G. and C. Kerenyi. *Essays on a Science of Mythology*. Tr. R. F. C. Hull. New York, 1949.

Kalevala. Tr. W. F. Kirby. New York, 1923. 2 vols.

Keith, A. Berriedale. *Indian Mythology*. Boston, 1917.

King, Jeff. *Where the Two Came to Their Father*. New York, 1943.

Kramer, Samuel Noah. *Sumerian Mythology*. Philadelphia, 1944.
——, ed. *Mythologies of the Ancient World*. Garden City, N. Y., 1961.
Krappe, Alexander Haggerty. *Études de mythologie et de folklore germanique*. Paris, 1928.
——. *The Science of Folklore*. New York, 1930.
——. *La Genèse des mythes*. Paris, 1938.
Krause, Aurel. *The Tlingit Indians*. Tr. Erna Gunther. Seattle, 1956.
LaBarre, Weston. *The Peyote Cult*. New Haven and Oxford, 1938.
Langdon, Stephen H. *Semitic Mythology*. Boston, 1931.
Larousse Encyclopedia of Mythology. New York, 1959.
Leland, Charles G. *The Algonquin Legends of New England*. Boston, 1898.
Lewin, Louis. *Les "paradis artificiels."* Paris, 1928.
——. *Phantastica*. London, 1931.
MacCulloch, John Arnott. *Celtic Mythology*. Boston, 1918.
——. *Eddic Mythology*. Boston, 1930.
MacDonnell, A. A. *Vedic Mythology*. Strasbourg, 1897.
MacKenzie, Donald A. *Myths from Melanesia and Indonesia*. London, n.d.
Maddox, John Lee. *The Medicine Man*. New York, 1923.
Makemson, Maud Worcester. *The Morning Star Rises*. New Haven, 1941.
Mason, J. Alden. *The Ancient Civilizations of Peru*. Penguin ed. 1957.
Maspero, Henri. "Légendes mythologiques dans le Chou King." *Journal asiatique*. vol. cciv. 1924.
Métraux, Alfred. *La Religion des Tupinamba*. Paris, 1928.
——. *Ethnology of Easter Island*. Bernice P. Bishop Museum Bulletin no. 160. Honolulu, 1940.
——. *Myths of the Toba and Pilaga Indians of the Gran Chaco*. Memoirs of the American Folklore Society, vol. 40. Philadelphia, 1946.
——. *Easter Island*. Tr. Michael Bullock. New York, 1957.
Moor, Edward. *The Hindu Pantheon*. London, 1810.
Morley, Sylvanus Griswold. *The Ancient Maya*. revised by George W. Brainerd, 3rd ed. Stanford, 1956.
Müller, W. Max. *Egyptian Mythology*. Boston, 1918.
Needham, Joseph. *Science and Civilization in China*. vol. iii. Cambridge (Eng.), 1959.
Neumann, Erich. *The Great Mother*. Tr. Ralph Mannheim. 1955.
Nihongi. Tr. W. G. Aston. London, 1896.
Nimuendaju, Curt. "The Tukuna." *University of California Publications in American Archaeology and Ethnology*, vol. 45. Berkeley, 1952.

Noble, Margaret E. and Ananda K. Coomaraswamy. *Myths of the Hindus and Buddhists.* Boston, n.d.

Nott, S. C. *The Mahabharata.* New York, 1956.

Parker, K. Langloh. *Australian Legendary Tales.* Ed. H. Drake Brockman. Sydney and London, 1953.

Parsons, Elsie Clews. *Pueblo Indian Religion.* 2 vols. Chicago, 1939.

Penzer, N. M., ed. *The Ocean of Story.* 10 vols. London, 1923 ff.

Petrullo, Vincenzo. *The Diabolic Root.* Philadelphia, 1934.

Plutarch. *Of Isis and Osiris.* Loeb ed.

Popol Vuh. English version by Delia Goetz and S. G. Morley from Spanish translation of Adrian Recinos. Norman, Okla., 1950.

Porte, Jean Baptiste F. V. *Recherches historiques sur les fêtes de la Tarasque.* (Aix), n.d.

Pritchard, James B. *Ancient Near Eastern Texts Relating to the Old Testament.* Princeton, 1955.

Radin, Paul. *The Trickster.* New York, 1956.

Raglan, Lord. *The Hero.* New York, 1956.

Ridgeway, William. *The Dramas and Dramatic Dances,* etc. Cambridge, 1915.

Rivers, W. H. R. *The Todas.* London, 1906.

Rugoff, Milton. *A Harvest of World Folktales.* New York, 1959.

Russian Fairy Tales. Tr. Norbert Guterman. Commentary by Roman Jakobson. New York, 1945.

Sachs, Hans. *World History of the Dance.* Tr. Bessie Schönberg. New York, 1952.

Sanders, N. K. *The Epic of Gilgamesh.* Penguin ed. 1960.

Saussure, Leopold de. *Les origines de l'astronomie chinoise.* Paris, 1930.

Schoolcraft, Henry Rowe. *Indian Legends from Algic Researches.* East Lansing, 1956.

Scott, Sir James George. *Indo-Chinese Mythology.* Boston, 1918.

Sebeok, Thomas A., ed. *Myth: A Symposium.* Bloomington, 1958.

Snorri Sturluson. *The Prose Edda.* Tr. A. G. Brodeur. New York and London, 1929.

Spence, Lewis. *The Outlines of Mythology.* Greenwich, Conn., 1961.

Spier, Leslie. "Southern Diegueño Customs." *University of California Publications in American Archaeology and Ethnology.* vol. 20. 1923.

Spinden, Herbert Joseph. *Maya Art and Civilization.* Indian Hills, Colo., 1957.

Stenberg, Molly Peacock. "The Peyote Culture Among the Wyoming Indians." *University of Wyoming Publications,* vol. 12. no. 4. Sept. 15, 1946.

Thompson, J. Eric. "Sky Bearers, Color and Directions in Maya and Mexican Religion." Carnegie Institution of Washington. Publication no. 436. *Contributions to American Archaeology,* vol. 2. no. 10. 1934.

——. "The Moon Goddess in Middle America." Carnegie Institution of Washington. Publication no. 509. *Contributions to Anthropology and History,* vol. v. no. 29, 1939.

Thompson, Stith. *Tales of the North American Indians.* Cambridge (Mass.), 1929.

Tirard, Helen Mary. *The Book of the Dead.* London, 1910.

Toor, Frances. *A Treasury of Mexican Folkways.* New York, 1947.

Troike, Rudolph C. "The Origin of Plains Mescalism." *American Anthropologist,* vol. 64. no. 5. Part I. October, 1962.

Vaillant, G. C. *The Aztecs of Mexico.* Penguin ed. 1951.

Wagley, Charles and Galvao, Eduardo. *The Tenetehara Indians of Brazil.* New York, 1949.

Waley, Arthur, tr. *The Book of Songs.* London, 1954. (2nd impr.)

Wasson, R. Gordon and Valentina P. *Russia, Mushrooms and History.* New York, 1952. 2 vols.

Wasson, R. Gordon. "Seeking the Magic Mushrooms." *Life,* May 13, 1957.

Waterman, T. T. "The Religious Practices of the Diegueño Indians." *University of California Publications in American Archaeology and Ethnology,* vol. 8. no. 6. Berkeley, 1908–10.

——. "The Paraphernalia of the Duwamish 'Spirit-Canoe' Ceremony." *Indian Notes,* vol. 7. no. 2. April, 1930.

Watts, Alan W. *Myth and Ritual in Christianity.* London and New York, 1954.

Webster, Hutton. *Rest Days.* New York, 1916.

Welsford, Enid. *The Court Masque.* Cambridge (Eng.), 1927.

Weyer, Edward Moffat. *The Eskimos.* New Haven, 1932.

Williamson, Robert W. *Religious and Cosmic Beliefs of Central Polynesia.* 2 vols. Cambridge (Eng.), 1933.

—— *Essays in Polynesian Anthropology.* Cambridge (Eng.), 1939.

Woolley, Sir Leonard. *Ur of the Chaldees.* Penguin ed. 1952.

INDEX